Mighty Mince Cookbook

Hamlyn Cookshelf Series

Mighty Mince Cookbook

Jane Todd

HAMLYN
London · New York · Sydney · Toronto

FOR ROBIN AND MITZI

The following titles are also available in this series:

Cooking with Yogurt · The Food Processor Cookbook
Potato Cookery · Sweets and Candies

The author and publishers would like to thank the following for their
help in sponsoring the colour photographs for this book:
Carmel Produce Information Bureau: page 104
Colman's Mustard: page 34
Mazola Pure Corn Oil: page 103
New Zealand Lamb Information Bureau: page 52
Pointerware (U.K.) Limited: page 51
R & C Vintners: page 33

Photography by Paul Williams
Front cover photograph by James Jackson
Illustrations by Robin Lawrie

First published in 1980 by The Hamlyn Publishing Group Limited
London · New York · Sydney · Toronto
Astronaut House, Feltham, Middlesex, England

This edition published in 1984
© Copyright The Hamlyn Publishing Group Limited 1980, 1984

ISBN 0 600 32415 X

Filmset in England by Photocomp Limited, Birmingham

Printed in Yugoslavia

Contents

Useful Facts and Figures

Notes on metrication

In this book quantities are given in metric and Imperial measures. Exact conversion from Imperial to metric measures does not usually give very convenient working quantities and so the metric measures have been rounded off into units of 25 grams. The table below shows the recommended equivalents.

Ounces	Approx g to nearest whole figure	Recommended conversion to nearest unit of 25	Ounces	Approx g to nearest whole figure	Recommended conversion to nearest unit of 25
1	28	25	11	312	300
2	57	50	12	340	350
3	85	75	13	368	375
4	113	100	14	396	400
5	142	150	15	425	425
6	170	175	16 (1 lb)	454	450
7	198	200	17	482	475
8	227	225	18	510	500
9	255	250	19	539	550
10	283	275	20 ($1\frac{1}{4}$ lb)	567	575

Note: When converting quantities over 20 oz first add the appropriate figures in the centre column, then adjust to the nearest unit of 25. As a general guide, 1 kg (1000 g) equals 2.2 lb or about 2 lb 3 oz. This method of conversion gives good results in nearly all cases, although in certain pastry and cake recipes a more accurate conversion is necessary to produce a balanced recipe.

Liquid measures The millilitre has been used in this book and the following table gives a few examples.

Imperial	Approx ml to nearest whole figure	Recommended ml	Imperial	Approx ml to nearest whole figure	Recommended ml
$\frac{1}{4}$ pint	142	150 ml	1 pint	567	600 ml
$\frac{1}{2}$ pint	283	300 ml	$1\frac{1}{2}$ pints	851	900 ml
$\frac{3}{4}$ pint	425	450 ml	$1\frac{3}{4}$ pints	992	1000 ml (1 litre)

Spoon measures All spoon measures given in this book are level unless otherwise stated.

Can sizes At present, cans are marked with the exact (usually to the nearest whole number) metric equivalent of the Imperial weight of the contents, so we have followed this practice when giving can sizes.

Oven temperatures

The table below gives recommended equivalents.

	°C	°F	Gas Mark		°C	°F	Gas Mark
Very cool	110	225	$\frac{1}{4}$	Moderately hot	190	375	5
	120	250	$\frac{1}{2}$		200	400	6
Cool	140	275	1	Hot	220	425	7
	150	300	2		230	450	8
Moderate	160	325	3	Very hot	240	475	9
	180	350	4				

Notes for American and Australian users

In America the 8-oz measuring cup is used. In Australia metric measures are now used in conjunction with the standard 250-ml measuring cup. The Imperial pint, used in Britain and Australia, is 20 fl oz, while the American pint is 16 oz. It is important to remember that the Australian tablespoon differs from both the British and American tablespoons; the table below gives a comparison. The British standard tablespoon, which has been used throughout this book, holds 17.7 ml, the American 14.2 ml, and the Australian 20 ml. A teaspoon holds approximately 5 ml in all three countries.

British	American	Australian
1 teaspoon	1 teaspoon	1 teaspoon
1 tablespoon	1 tablespoon	1 tablespoon
2 tablespoons	3 tablespoons	2 tablespoons
$3\frac{1}{2}$ tablespoons	5 tablespoons	3 tablespoons
4 tablespoons	5 tablespoons	$3\frac{1}{2}$ tablespoons

An Imperial/American guide to solid and liquid measures

Imperial	American	Imperial	American
Solid measures		**Liquid measures**	
1 lb butter or		$\frac{1}{4}$ pint liquid	$\frac{2}{3}$ cup liquid
margarine	2 cups	$\frac{1}{2}$ pint	$1\frac{1}{4}$ cups
1 lb flour	4 cups	$\frac{3}{4}$ pint	2 cups
1 lb granulated		1 pint	$2\frac{1}{2}$ cups
or castor sugar	2 cups	$1\frac{1}{2}$ pints	$3\frac{3}{4}$ cups
1 lb icing sugar	3 cups	2 pints	5 cups ($2\frac{1}{2}$ pints)
8 oz rice	1 cup		

Note: When making any of the recipes in this book, only follow one set of measurements as they are not interchangeable.

Introduction

Minced meat was certainly not invented by school cooks as a means of nourishing their charges or as a way to utilise the remains of the Sunday joint. Sadly, this is often how many people were first introduced to it and who can blame them for being put off for life?

My research reveals that the Chinese and Arabs were adept at utilising the less choice parts of the animal which they pulverised (mincers and food processors hadn't been thought of). Then spices and seasonings were added, no doubt to mask the flavour of the meat, and the mixture turned into meatballs. According to my edition of *Mrs Beeton's All About Cookery* published in 1911, mincemeat was just that, with the addition of currants, apples, spices and seasonings, and the mixture was used as a filling for pies. The recipe, based on 2 lb minced beef, cost about 10d per pound.

Undoubtedly today minced beef is one of the most versatile and cheapest forms of protein and can be made, with a little care and the subtle use of herbs, spices and seasonings, into an exciting range of dishes suitable for family fare, buffet meals for a crowd or for entertaining. I never hesitate to serve my guests a moussaka, lasagne, or in the summer home-made hamburgers cooked over the barbecue. These dishes are easy to prepare, even easier on the pocket and seem to be well appreciated.

Beef is not the only kind of minced meat to be used – lamb, pork and veal all have a place in the *Mighty Mince Cookbook* and you'll find recipes using all these meats. Before you try any of the recipes read the first chapter where there are many tips and hints on buying, mincing, storing, freezing and cooking minced meats. The recipes range from starters through to hamburgers, main course dishes, fork fare for a crowd and traditional minced dishes from around the world. Devotee as I am of minced meats, I certainly don't advocate that you serve them morning, noon and night, or as a starter and the main course for any one meal.

Please don't spurn minced meat – I hope that by looking through this book and trying some of the recipes you will agree with me that it is one of the most versatile and economical choices the butcher can offer.

Jane Todd

All About Minced Meats

All the recipes in this book call for *raw* minced meat – beef, veal, pork, lamb or a mixture of these meats. Minced beef is obviously the most readily available, but if you cultivate your local butcher and don't want just 1 lb minced meat you'll find that more likely than not he will mince whatever you require. For certain recipes – hamburgers and steak tartare – I'm in favour of mincing the meat at home. This way you can control the proportion of fat to lean and can specify the cut; chuck, leg, shin and clod are all good cuts of beef for mincing at home, but steak tartare requires fillet or rump. Pork belly is good but must be mixed with a leaner cut; for mincing veal I buy pie veal and for lamb any boneless cut will do. Another advantage of home mincing is that you can put the meat through the mincer several times, thus improving the texture. In fact for the Turkish kebabs recipe finely minced meat is essential to achieve the correct consistency. You can also put the onions through the mincer as well to save chopping or grating them, but if you buy ready-minced meat I see no advantage in fixing up the mincer just for the onions. The price of minced beef does vary and often a butcher will display three grades sometimes labelled minced beef, ground beef and minced steak. Generally speaking, ground beef is more finely minced and minced steak has a lower proportion of fat. At all costs reject minced beef which looks as if it contains a high proportion of fat and is discoloured.

The Mincer

If you know you are going to mince a lot of meat at home, then it is worth investing in a mincer attachment which you can buy for certain larger electric mixers; a blender won't mince raw meat satisfactorily but a food processor will do an admirable job. Failing that, the clamp-on hand mincer is excellent and you can

mince the meat finely or coarsely. Do make sure you trim away all the gristle and skin from the meat prior to putting it through the mincer otherwise you'll begin to wish that you had purchased ready-made minced meat – the gristle gets entwined around the coil and you have to dismantle the whole lot and start again.

Storing Minced Meats

All minced meats should be cooked on the day of purchase. Due to the number of exposed surfaces minced meat does deteriorate more quickly than any other cut of meat. There's no danger in preparing and cooking a dish the day before it is required, providing that it is cooled quickly and stored overnight in the refrigerator. On the question of reheating, it is perfectly safe to do so if you follow the basic rules of hygiene – store the dish in the refrigerator, use it within a day and reheat it thoroughly, don't just show it the oven.

Using the Freezer

Buying or mincing meat in bulk for the freezer is an advantage providing it is packed in usable quantities. There's no point in freezing a huge mound of minced beef if all you ever require at any one time is 1 lb. I find it an advantage too to freeze raw hamburgers and meatballs.

Most made-up dishes freeze satisfactorily, and with a stock of lasagne and moussaka in the freezer the family won't starve, but I do think there is a difference between the freshly prepared and frozen varieties.

The Use of Extenders

The most commonly used extender (or stretcher) to minced meat is soya. This you can buy at health food stores and supermarkets and in certain recipes – mainly the casserole-type ones – it is virtually undetectable. I would recommend that you use no more than one-quarter of the amount of soya to minced meat. A meat and soya mixture does not shrink so much during cooking as 100 % meat, and of course there is a cost saving.

Bread or breadcrumbs can also be used as an extender. In most meatball and meat loaf recipes bread is usually added to give a firmer and less crumbly texture. Fresh breadcrumbs can be used or bread soaked in milk or water and then squeezed dry.

Herbs and Spices

The subtle use of herbs and spices does wonders for most dishes, but they are particularly good in minced meat dishes. The recipes in this book recommend fresh and dried herbs: I think the former are infinitely better but I know it isn't always possible, particularly in winter, to have fresh herbs to hand. If a recipe states fresh herbs and you only have dried available use half the quantity stated for fresh. Dried herbs are much stronger and more pungent and can dominate the flavour of the cooked dish. Both herbs and spices are used to complement the basic ingredient and must never be overpowering. Again, freshly grated spices have a better flavour than the ground varieties. I have recently discovered that you can buy spices in a container like a pepper mill and grind them as you need them. A pepper mill is a must as the flavour of freshly ground black or white peppercorns bears no comparison to that of the dusty powder in small drums. In most cases I suggest the use of freshly ground black pepper except in a white sauce or similar recipe where the black specks of pepper spoil the appearance.

Barbecues

The taste of home-made hamburgers cooked over the bar-becue is out of this world. Apart from hamburgers, meatballs, home-made sausages and Turkish kebabs served with garlic or herb bread and a selection of salads, all make good barbecue fare, and a barbecue is a delightful way to entertain during the warmer weather. It's easy on the cook, as it's surprising how many willing helpers there seem to be when the cooking is done out of doors! Washing up can be kept to a minimum if you don't object to paper plates.

2
Appetisers and Starters

Minced meat can be used to make a surprisingly wide variety of first course dishes from the more substantial pâtés and terrines to the quick-to-prepare cocktail meatballs which can be served with dips. The pâtés and terrines can also be served as a lunch or picnic dish. You'll find that the soup recipes are very hearty and accompanied by chunks of crusty bread could be a meal in themselves.

Do remember to give your food eye appeal – it's a particularly important point with minced dishes. The terrines and pâtés can be garnished with bay leaves, watercress, raw carrot sticks, gherkin fans or olives, but please don't overdo it – that's almost as bad as naked food! Soups benefit from a generous sprinkling of freshly chopped parsley or chives.

Cocktail Meatballs with Barbecue Dip

450 g / 1 lb minced beef
1 onion, grated
50 g / 2 oz fresh white breadcrumbs
salt and freshly ground black pepper
2 tablespoons chopped parsley
1 egg, lightly beaten
2 tablespoons oil
Barbecue Dip
25 g / 1 oz butter
1 onion, chopped
1 (227-g / 8-oz) can tomatoes
50 g / 2 oz stoned green olives
1 teaspoon dry mustard
few drops of Tabasco sauce
1 teaspoon Worcestershire sauce

First prepare the barbecue dip. Heat the butter in a frying pan and sauté the onion until softened. Add the remaining ingredients and simmer for 15 minutes. Allow the mixture to cool slightly, then blend in a liquidiser (or press through a sieve). Pour into a serving bowl and leave to cool.

To make the meatballs, mix together the beef, onion, breadcrumbs, seasoning and parsley and bind with the lightly beaten egg. With floured hands, shape the mixture into 2.5-cm / 1-inch balls. Heat the oil in a frying pan and cook the meatballs for about 5 minutes, turning them with a pair of tongs so that they are well-browned on all sides. Drain on absorbent paper.

Insert a cocktail stick into each meatball and place on a tray with the bowl of barbecue dip. *Makes about 30*

Cocktail Meatballs with Spicy Dip

450 g / 1 lb minced beef
1 onion, grated
salt and freshly ground black pepper
1 egg, lightly beaten
Spicy Dip
1½ tablespoons cornflour
3 tablespoons wine vinegar
1 tablespoon Worcestershire sauce
2 tablespoons tomato purée
300 ml/½ pint dry cider
pinch of chilli powder
1 clove garlic, crushed
2 carrots, grated
2 teaspoons castor sugar

Mix together the beef, onion and seasoning. Bind the mixture together with the lightly beaten egg. With floured hands, shape the mixture into walnut-sized balls and place, in a single layer, in a lightly oiled roasting tin. Cook in a moderately hot oven (200°C, 400°F, Gas Mark 6) for 20 minutes.

To make the dip, blend the cornflour and vinegar in a saucepan. Add the remaining ingredients and, stirring, bring the mixture to the boil. Simmer for 5 minutes.

Place the hot meatballs on a serving dish and spear each one with a cocktail stick. Serve the dip, either hot or cold, in a separate bowl. *Makes about 35*

Lamb Meatballs with Cream and Caraway Dip

450 g / 1 lb minced lamb
2 teaspoons ground cumin
3 teaspoons chopped fresh mint
2 spring onions, chopped
salt and freshly ground black pepper
25 g / 1 oz fresh white breadcrumbs
1 egg, lightly beaten
Cream and Caraway Dip
2 (142-ml/5-fl oz) cartons soured cream
1 teaspoon caraway seeds

Mix together the lamb, cumin, mint, spring onions, seasoning and breadcrumbs. Bind the mixture together with the lightly beaten egg. With floured hands, shape the mixture into 2.5-cm/1-inch meatballs. Place them in a greased roasting tin and cook in a hot oven (220°C, 425°F, Gas Mark 7) for 15 minutes, until well browned.

Meanwhile mix together the soured cream and caraway seeds. Spoon the dip into a serving bowl placed on a large plate or tray. Arrange the meatballs around the bowl. Serve cocktail sticks to spear the meatballs for dunking into the dip.
Makes about 30

Variation

The caraway seeds may be replaced by 3-4 tablespoons snipped chives to make a cream and chive dip.

Stuffed Tomatoes

Stuffed tomatoes make a good summer starter. If you have fresh herbs to hand, the addition of a tablespoon of chopped marjoram or basil will enhance the filling.

4 large tomatoes
25 g / 1 oz butter
2 spring onions, chopped
50 g / 2 oz mushrooms, chopped
100 g / 4 oz minced ham
2 tablespoons fresh white breadcrumbs
2 tablespoons chopped parsley
salt and freshly ground black pepper

Slice the tops off the tomatoes and with a teaspoon carefully scoop out the insides taking care not to split the cases.

Heat the butter in a frying pan and sauté the spring onions until softened. Add the mushrooms and sauté for a further 2-3 minutes. Stir in the tomato pulp, ham, breadcrumbs, parsley and seasoning.

Fill the tomato cases with the ham mixture and replace the tops. Cook in a moderate oven (180°C, 350°F, Gas Mark 4) for 20 minutes. Serve hot or cold. *Serves 4*

Stuffed Mushrooms

4 large mushrooms
25 g / 1 oz butter
100 g / 4 oz minced pork
grated rind of 1 lemon
salt and freshly ground black pepper
1 tablespoon fresh white breadcrumbs
2 tablespoons chopped fresh sage
olive oil
Garnish
watercress

Wipe the mushrooms with a damp cloth, trim off the stalks and chop them finely. Heat the butter in a frying pan and sauté the mushroom stalks for a few minutes. Stir in the pork and sauté for about 5 minutes, until evenly browned. Stir in the lemon rind, seasoning, breadcrumbs and sage.

Place the mushroom caps on a greased baking sheet and brush them with a little olive oil. Divide the pork filling between the mushrooms and cook in a moderate oven (160°C, 325°F, Gas Mark 3) for 15-20 minutes.

Place each filled mushroom on a small serving plate, garnish with watercress and serve hot.

Pork Terrine

(Illustrated on page 33)

A terrine makes a good meal starter providing the main course isn't too substantial. With crusty French bread and a salad a terrine is ideal served for lunch or supper. Do ensure that it is served chilled – the cooked dish will keep for 3-4 days in the refrigerator.

225 g / 8 oz minced pork
225 g / 8 oz minced veal
1 small onion, chopped
1 tablespoon chopped fresh sage
2 tablespoons chopped parsley
1 clove garlic, crushed
100 g / 4 oz mushrooms, chopped
salt and freshly ground black pepper
2 eggs
4 rashers streaky bacon
2 bay leaves

Mix together the pork, veal, onion, herbs, garlic, mushrooms and plenty of seasoning. Lightly beat the eggs and mix into the meat mixture.

Grease a 1.5-litre / 2½-pint ovenproof dish or terrine and pack the mixture in. Remove the bacon rinds, stretch the rashers and lay them across the top of the mixture. Place the bay leaves on top of the bacon. Cover closely with a piece of greased greaseproof paper or a butter paper, then cover with a lid or a piece of foil.

Place the dish in a roasting tin and pour in water to come halfway up the outside of the dish. Cook in a moderate oven (180°C, 350°F, Gas Mark 4) for about 1½ hours, or until the juice from the terrine is clear.

Remove from the oven, take off the coverings and leave to cool at room temperature, then chill in the refrigerator.

Serve from the dish. *Serves 6-8 as a starter, 4-6 as a lunch or supper dish*

Pork and Olive Pâté

4 spring onions, chopped
450 g/1 lb minced pork
225 g/8 oz sausagemeat
1 tablespoon chopped fresh sage
12 pimiento-stuffed olives, sliced
salt and freshly ground black pepper
4 tablespoons dry cider
Garnish
tomato slices
chopped parsley

Mix together the spring onions, pork, sausagemeat, sage, olives and plenty of seasoning.

Blend the mixture with the cider and pack it into a greased 450-g/1-lb loaf tin. Cook in a moderate oven (180°C, 350°F, Gas Mark 4) for $1\frac{1}{4}$ hours.

Leave to cool, weighted, in the tin. Turn out on to a serving dish and garnish with tomato slices and a sprinkling of chopped parsley.

Serve with toast or French bread. *Serves 6*

Country Pâté

450 g / 1 lb minced beef
450 g / 1 lb streaky bacon, minced
175 g / 6 oz fresh white breadcrumbs
1 teaspoon ground allspice
1 teaspoon ground nutmeg
salt and freshly ground black pepper
1 egg, lightly beaten
6 tablespoons red wine
2 bay leaves
300 ml / $\frac{1}{2}$ pint aspic
Garnish
watercress

Mix together the beef, bacon and breadcrumbs. Add the spices and seasoning and blend the mixture together with the lightly beaten egg and wine.

Pack the mixture into a greased 1-kg/2-lb loaf tin. Place the bay leaves on top. Cover with foil and cook in a moderate oven (180°C, 350°F, Gas Mark 4) for $1\frac{3}{4}$ hours.

Remove from the oven and leave to cool, weighted.

When cold turn on to a serving dish and coat with the aspic. Leave to set and garnish with watercress.

Serve with French bread or toast. *Serves 8*

Beef Soup

Served with garlic or herb bread this hearty soup makes a satisfying lunch-time dish.

2 slices white bread
150 ml/$\frac{1}{4}$ pint milk
50 g/2 oz butter
1 onion, chopped
1 clove garlic, crushed
225 g/8 oz minced beef
$\frac{1}{2}$ teaspoon dried mixed herbs
2 tablespoons chopped parsley
salt and freshly ground pepper
2 eggs, lightly beaten
1$\frac{1}{4}$ litres/2$\frac{1}{2}$ pints beef stock
Garnish
chopped parsley

Remove the crusts from the bread and break the bread into a bowl. Pour on the milk and leave to soak for 15 minutes.

Heat a quarter of the butter in a frying pan and sauté the onion and garlic for about 5 minutes, until softened.

Squeeze the milk from the bread and mix the bread with the beef, herbs, seasoning, onion and garlic. Bind the mixture with the lightly beaten eggs and mix thoroughly. With floured hands, shape into small meatballs.

Heat the remaining butter in a frying pan and sauté the meatballs until browned on all sides. Drain on absorbent paper.

Meanwhile bring the beef stock to the boil. Add the meatballs, lower the heat and simmer for 10 minutes.

Serve the soup garnished with plenty of chopped parsley.
Serves 4-6

Mexican Soup

This is another hearty winter soup which is a meal in itself.
The beans and chick peas need to be soaked overnight.

225 g/8 oz dried chick peas
225 g/8 oz dried red kidney beans
2 tablespoons oil
1 onion, chopped
225 g/8 oz minced beef
1 green pepper, seeded and chopped
1 (425-g/15-oz) can tomatoes
450 ml/$\frac{3}{4}$ pint beef stock
$\frac{1}{2}$ teaspoon chilli powder
pinch of salt

Place the chick peas and kidney beans together in a bowl and cover with cold water. Leave to soak overnight.

Heat the oil in a pan and sauté the onion until softened. Add the minced beef and cook, stirring until browned. Add the pepper, tomatoes with their juice, drained chick peas and beans, stock, chilli powder and salt. Bring to the boil, cover and simmer for 30 minutes. Cool slightly, then blend in a liquidiser. Reheat (the soup should be thick) and serve with hot garlic or herb bread. *Serves 4*

Italian Meatball Soup

Another hearty main-course soup.

75 g/3 oz butter
1 carrot, sliced
2 potatoes, cubed
1 stick celery, chopped
1 onion, chopped
1 (227-g/8-oz) can tomatoes
2 tablespoons tomato purée
900 ml/1½ pints beef stock
salt and freshly ground black pepper
¼ teaspoon dried oregano
pinch of sugar
350 g/12 oz minced beef
1 clove garlic, crushed
1 small egg, lightly beaten
To Serve
grated Parmesan cheese

Heat 50 g/2 oz of the butter in a large saucepan and sauté the carrot, potatoes, celery and onion for 5 minutes. Add the canned tomatoes with their juice, the tomato purée, stock, seasoning, oregano and pinch of sugar. Bring to the boil, cover and simmer for 30 minutes.

Meanwhile mix the minced beef and garlic together, adding plenty of seasoning, and bind with the lightly beaten egg. With floured hands, shape the mixture into small meatballs. Sauté them in the remaining butter until browned on all sides. Drain on absorbent paper.

Add the meatballs to the soup and simmer for a further 10 minutes. Ladle the soup into bowls and serve sprinkled with Parmesan cheese. *Serves 4*

3

Hamburgers

A perfectly cooked and presented hamburger is one of the world's finest dishes, but sadly we have been led to believe, through the efforts of some eating houses, that a burger is about as thick as a 10p piece and tastes like cotton wool. Happily that situation is now being rectified and we can obtain the real thing this side of the Atlantic.

Hamburgers are one of the easiest and quickest minced dishes to make at home and can be served in or out of a bun. It is essential to select the best quality minced beef – or better still to mince it yourself not too far in advance. A true hamburger is pure meat with no additions other than salt and pepper and perhaps some chopped parsley – no self-respecting American would bind a hamburger with beaten egg or stretch the meat with breadcrumbs or soya. Another important point is that when making hamburgers they should be handled as little as possible. Over-handling makes them tough.

All minced dishes are enhanced by garnishes and accompaniments, but here the hamburger really comes into its own as there is really no limit to the accompaniments you can select to complement and serve alongside a burger. You can also dress up your burgers (in or out of a bun) with an enormous variety of different toppings – try fried onions, a pineapple ring, a dollop of cottage cheese or soured cream, crumbled blue cheese, a slice of mature Cheddar cheese or one of the savoury butters on page 42.

The Basic Hamburger

This is what any American would expect when he asked for a hamburger! And it is a far cry from the so-called burgers available in many eating houses. There are of course infinite variations, but the basic essential is freshly minced, good quality beef.

4 baps or sesame seed rolls
450 g/1 lb minced beef
salt and freshly ground black pepper
50 g/2 oz butter
1 tablespoon oil

Place the baps on a baking sheet and heat through in a moderate oven (180°C, 350°F, Gas Mark 4) for 10 minutes.

Mix the beef with plenty of seasoning. Divide the beef into four equal-sized portions and shape each one into a round, flat cake. (Avoid over-handling the meat.)

Heat the butter and oil together in a frying pan large enough to take all four burgers at the same time. Cook the burgers over a moderate heat for 3 minutes on each side – this gives a medium-rare hamburger.

Slit the baps and place a burger in each one. Serve at once with a selection of the following – ketchup, chilli sauce, mixed pickles, piccalilli, chopped raw onions, chopped red and green peppers or any of the accompaniments given on page 41.
Serves 4

Note An alternative method of cooking burgers is to cook them dry in sea salt which surprisingly enough doesn't make them too salty and gives a nice crust to the burger.

Sprinkle a heavy-based frying pan with an even layer of sea salt and heat until it begins to brown. Add the burgers and cook as above.

Hamburgers with Cream and Wine Sauce

This is a dish which I wouldn't hesitate to serve at a dinner party, but I do recommend that you buy braising steak and mince it yourself. Ideal accompaniments would be a green or mixed salad and potatoes tossed in butter, chives and parsley.

1 kg / 2 lb minced beef
salt and freshly ground black pepper
2 tablespoons oil
25 g / 1 oz butter
Sauce
1 small onion, finely chopped
150 ml / $\frac{1}{4}$ pint red wine
3 tablespoons double cream
1 tablespoon tomato purée
2-3 tablespoons chopped parsley
Garnish
watercress sprigs

Mix the beef with plenty of seasoning. Divide the beef into six equal-sized portions and shape each one into a round, flat (but not too thin) cake.

Heat the oil and butter together in a frying pan large enough to accommodate all the burgers at once. When very hot add the burgers and cook for 3-4 minutes on each side, depending on how rare you prefer them. Transfer the burgers to a heated serving dish and keep warm.

Spoon all but about 1 tablespoon of the oil out of the pan. Return to the heat and sauté the onion for about 5 minutes, until softened. Pour in the wine, increase the heat and with a wooden spoon stir the base of the pan to scrape up the sediment and pan juices. Boil for about 1 minute. Remove from the heat, stir in the cream, tomato purée and parsley. Reheat, but do not boil, and pour over the burgers.

Garnish with sprigs of watercress and serve at once.*Serves 6*

Burgers with Pizzaiola Sauce

1 kg/2 lb minced beef
salt and freshly ground black pepper
Sauce
1 tablespoon oil
2 onions, chopped
2 cloves garlic, crushed
1 green pepper, seeded and chopped
1 red pepper, seeded and chopped
50 g/2 oz button mushrooms, sliced
1 (425-g/15-oz) can tomatoes
1 teaspoon dried marjoram
salt and freshly ground black pepper
few drops of Tabasco sauce

Mix the beef with plenty of seasoning. Divide the beef into six equal-sized portions and shape each one into a round, flat cake.

To make the sauce, heat the oil in a pan and sauté the onions and garlic until softened. Add the peppers and cook for a further 10 minutes. Stir in the mushrooms, tomatoes, marjoram, seasoning and Tabasco sauce. Cover and simmer for 30 minutes.

Preheat the grill and cook the burgers under the grill for 4-5 minutes on each side, depending on how rare you prefer them. Arrange the burgers on a heated serving dish and pour over the sauce. *Serves 6*

Hamburgers au Poivre

Since fillet steak is fast becoming a figment of our imaginations, this recipe using best quality minced beef makes an equally good dinner party dish.

1 kg/2 lb minced beef
2 tablespoons whole black peppercorns
1 tablespoon oil
50 g/2 oz butter
2 tablespoons brandy
150 ml/¼ pint double cream
3 tablespoons chopped parsley
salt

Divide the beef into six equal-sized portions and shape each one into a round, flat cake.

Grind the peppercorns coarsely using a pestle and mortar or place them in a polythene bag and crush with a rolling pin. Press the crushed peppercorns into each side of the burgers and set aside for 30 minutes.

Heat the oil and butter together in a frying pan large enough to accommodate all the burgers at once. Add the burgers and cook for 3-4 minutes on each side, depending on how rare you prefer them. Transfer the burgers to a heated serving dish and keep warm.

Add the brandy to the pan, heat and ignite. Draw the pan off the heat and stir in the cream and parsley. Season the sauce with salt, reheat, but do not boil, and pour out over the burgers.

Serve with a salad. *Serves 6*

Hamburgers with Dill

1 kg/2 lb minced beef
2 tablespoons chopped fresh dill
salt and freshly ground black pepper
75 g/3 oz butter
2 tablespoons chopped parsley
juice of 1 lemon
sea salt
few drops each of Worcestershire and Tabasco sauces
Garnish
watercress

Mix together the beef, dill and seasoning. Divide the mixture into six equal-sized portions and shape each one into a flat, round cake.

Mix together the butter and parsley with a little of the lemon juice. Shape into a roll and wrap in cling film. Leave to chill in the refrigerator.

Sprinkle a heavy-based frying pan with an even layer of sea salt and heat until it begins to brown. Add the burgers and cook for 3-4 minutes on each side, depending on how rare you prefer them.

Arrange the burgers on a heated serving dish and sprinkle each one with a little lemon juice and a few drops of Worcestershire and Tabasco sauces. Top each one with a portion of parsley butter. Garnish with watercress and serve at once. *Serves 6*

Mexican Burgers

675 g/1½ lb minced beef
freshly ground black pepper
pinch of ground cumin
pinch of garlic salt
4 spring onions, chopped
Guacamole
1 large avocado
3 tablespoons lemon juice
1 clove garlic, crushed
salt and freshly ground white pepper
Garnish
shredded white cabbage
lemon wedges

Mix together the beef, black pepper, cumin, garlic, salt and spring onions. Divide the mixture into four equal-sized portions and shape each one into a round, flat cake.

To make the guacamole, halve the avocado, discard the stone and scoop the flesh into a bowl. Mash with a fork and mix with the lemon juice, garlic and seasoning.

Preheat the grill and cook the burgers for 4-5 minutes on each side, depending on how rare you prefer them.

Place the shredded cabbage on a serving dish and top with the burgers. On each burger, place a spoonful of guacamole and top with a lemon wedge. *Serves 4*

Pork terrine (see page 20)

Cheese-crowned Burgers

675 g/1½ lb minced beef
2 tablespoons chopped parsley
salt and freshly ground black pepper
1 onion, grated
few drops of Tabasco sauce
4 slices French bread
butter
French mustard
4 slices cheese
4 lettuce leaves
2 tomatoes, sliced
4 gherkins

Mix together the beef, parsley, seasoning, onion and Tabasco sauce. Divide the mixture into four equal-sized portions and shape each one into a round, flat cake.

Lightly toast the slices of French bread, spread with butter and French mustard and keep warm.

Preheat the grill and cook the burgers for 4-5 minutes on each side, depending on how rare you prefer them. Place a slice of cheese on each burger and grill until the cheese begins to melt.

On each slice of toast place a lettuce leaf and some tomato slices. Add a burger to each portion and top with a gherkin.
Serves 4

A selection of burgers: (from the top) grilled blue cheese; Mexican; wine-glazed; with pizzaiola sauce; cheese-crowned

Grilled Blue Cheese Burgers

100 g/4 oz Danish blue cheese
1.5 kg/3 lb minced beef
4 spring onions, finely chopped
1 teaspoon Worcestershire sauce
salt and freshly ground black pepper
pinch of dry mustard
12 baps

Crumble the cheese into a bowl and mix in the beef, onions, Worcestershire sauce, seasoning and mustard. Cover with cling film and leave in the refrigerator for at least 1 hour to allow the flavours to blend.

Divide the mixture into 12 equal-sized portions and shape each one into a round, flat cake.

Preheat the grill and cook the burgers for 4-5 minutes on each side, depending on how rare you prefer them.

Serve the burgers in warmed baps with a selection of hamburger accompaniments. *Serves 12*

Wine-glazed Burgers

675 g/1½ lb minced beef
2 tablespoons chopped parsley
salt and freshly ground black pepper
1 tablespoon oil
50 g/2 oz butter
2 baps
4 spring onions, chopped
1 clove garlic, crushed
½ teaspoon French mustard
150 ml/¼ pint red wine
Garnish
parsley sprigs

Mix together the beef, parsley and seasoning to taste. Divide the mixture into four equal-sized portions and shape each one into a round, flat cake.

Heat the oil and butter together in a frying pan and fry the burgers for 4-5 minutes on each side, depending on how rare you prefer them. Lift out the burgers and keep warm in a cool oven (140°C, 275°F, Gas Mark 1). Put the baps in the oven to heat through.

Add the onions, garlic and mustard to the pan and sauté for 2-3 minutes, stirring. Pour in the wine and boil until reduced by half.

To serve, cut the baps in half and place a burger on each half. Arrange on a serving dish and spoon some of the wine sauce over each burger. Serve garnished with parsley sprigs and with a selection of hamburger accompaniments. *Serves 4*

Baked Burgers

675 g/1½ lb minced beef
salt and freshly ground black pepper
2 tablespoons oil
2 onions, sliced
6 baps

Mix the beef with plenty of seasoning and divide the beef into six equal-sized portions. Shape each portion into a round, flat cake. Place in a lightly oiled roasting tin and cook in a moderately hot oven (190°C, 375°F, Gas Mark 5) for 15-25 minutes, depending on how rare you prefer the burgers.

Meanwhile heat the oil in a frying pan and sauté the onions until softened and lightly browned.

Heat the baps and pop a burger, topped with some fried onions, in each one. Serve with a selection of hamburger accompaniments. *Serves 6*

Bacon Burgers

450 g / 1 lb minced beef
2 tablespoons chopped parsley
salt and freshly ground black pepper
4 rashers streaky bacon
Dijon mustard
1 tablespoon oil
50 g/2 oz butter
4 finger rolls

Mix together the beef and parsley with plenty of seasoning. Divide the mixture into four equal-sized portions and shape each one into a sausage shape.

Remove the bacon rinds and stretch the rashers. Spread each one on one side with some mustard. Wrap a mustard-spread rasher around each burger and secure it with a wooden cocktail stick.

Heat the oil and butter together in a frying pan and fry the burgers for about 8-10 minutes, turning them to brown on all sides. Remove the cocktail sticks.

Slit the rolls and put a bacon-wrapped burger in each one. Serve with a selection of hamburger accompaniments. *Serves 4*

Peanut Burgers

675 g / 1½ lb minced beef
1 onion, grated
25 g / 1 oz unsalted peanuts, chopped
1 teaspoon Worcestershire sauce
1 tablespoon peanut butter
salt and freshly ground black pepper

Mix together the beef and onion, then blend in the remaining ingredients with seasoning to taste. Divide the mixture into four equal-sized portions and shape each one into a round, flat cake.

Preheat the grill and cook the burgers for 4-5 minutes on each side, depending on how rare you prefer them.

Serve on their own, or in a bap, with a selection of hamburger accompaniments. *Serves 4*

Hamburger Accompaniments

Hamburgers are normally served with a selection of accompaniments ranging from sauces and relishes to chopped onions, peppers and tomatoes.

You don't have to prepare your own accompaniment – you can if you prefer serve a selection of commercially-prepared ones – try mixed pickles, piccalilli, tomato ketchup, corn or green pepper relish, chilli sauces, mustards, gherkins or olives.

For those who prefer to make their own here are some quick-to-prepare sauces and relishes.

Danish Blue Sauce

Crumble 50 g/2 oz Danish blue cheese into a bowl and mix in 150 ml/¼ pint soured cream, 1 tablespoon grated onion and a few drops of lemon juice. Chill before serving.

Peanut Sauce

Sauté a chopped onion and a crushed clove of garlic in 50 g/2 oz butter until softened. Stir in 1 tablespoon Worcestershire sauce, 3 tablespoons peanut butter and 1 tablespoon lemon juice. Chill, then stir in 150 ml/¼ pint soured cream.

Creamy Horseradish Sauce

Lightly whip 150 ml/¼ pint double cream and stir in 2 table-spoons wine vinegar, 3 tablespoons grated fresh horseradish, 2 tablespoons chopped parsley or chives and a pinch of salt and white pepper.

Pepper Relish

Sauté 2 seeded and chopped green peppers and a chopped onion in 50 g/2 oz butter until softened. Add 4 tablespoons white vinegar, 4 peeled and chopped tomatoes, a few drops of Tabasco sauce and salt and pepper to taste. Bring to the boil and simmer for 10 minutes. Serve cold.

Flavoured Butters

To ring the changes with the basic hamburger try these flavoured butters. They can be made in advance and will keep in the refrigerator for up to 2 weeks.

The garlic and herb butters can also be used to flavour hot French bread to serve as an accompaniment. Slice a French loaf, diagonally, almost through to the base. Spread the flavoured butter on to each side of each slice – a small palette knife is best for this – wrap the loaf in foil and heat it in a moderately hot oven (190°C, 375°F, Gas Mark 5) for 10 minutes.

Basic Butter

100 g/4 oz unsalted butter
1 tablespoon chopped parsley
2 teaspoons lemon juice
1 teaspoon grated lemon rind

Beat the butter with a wooden spoon until softened. Mix in the parsley, lemon juice and rind. Spoon on to a piece of foil or greaseproof paper and pat into a log shape.

Fold the foil over the butter and roll into a neater shape. Chill in the refrigerator.

To use, cut into slices and place a slice on top of a burger just before serving.

Variations

Herb Butter To the basic butter add 1 tablespoon chopped chives and 1 teaspoon each of chopped fresh thyme, sage and tarragon.
Garlic Butter Omit the parsley from the basic butter and blend in 2-3 cloves crushed garlic.
Curry Butter To the basic butter add 1 teaspoon curry paste, salt, freshly ground black pepper and a pinch of paprika.
Blue Cheese Butter To the basic butter add 100 g/4 oz crumbled Danish blue cheese.
Mustard Butter To the basic butter add 2 tablespoons of your favourite made mustard – French, German or English.
Mint Butter To the basic butter add 2 tablespoons chopped fresh mint.

4

Main Course Dishes

Here you will find a selection of dishes using beef, lamb, pork, veal and a mixture of meats suitable to serve as main course dishes for the family.

Do bear in mind that the presentation of a dish is as equally important as the preparation and cooking of it and that a simple garnish of chopped parsley will do wonders for many minced dishes which otherwise may look unappealing. Pastry dishes can be cheered up with a garnish of sprigs of watercress or parsley.

When planning your family menus try to ring the changes with the accompaniments and instead of potatoes serve either rice or pasta which are much easier for the cook as neither have to be peeled! With dishes such as the Cheesy cottage pie which includes potatoes, just serve a seasonal vegetable as the accompaniment. Jacket potatoes and a crunchy cabbage and carrot salad are very good served with the casserole-type dishes as they give the necessary contrast in texture and colour.

A final reminder: should there be any of the dish left over do cool it quickly and store in the refrigerator, lightly covered with cling film. Use it up within a day, making sure that it is thoroughly reheated.

Hungarian Minced Beef

(Illustrated on page 51)

1 tablespoon oil
2 onions, sliced
1 clove garlic, crushed
450 g/1 lb minced beef
2 teaspoons flour
1 tablespoon paprika
1 green pepper, seeded and chopped
1 (227-g/8-oz) can tomatoes
salt and freshly ground black pepper
150 ml/$\frac{1}{4}$ pint beef stock
1 (142-ml/5-fl oz) carton soured cream or natural yogurt

Heat the oil in a flameproof casserole and sauté the onions and garlic for about 5 minutes, until lightly browned. Add the beef and cook, stirring to break up the lumps, until nicely browned. Stir in the flour and cook for a further 1-2 minutes. Add the paprika, green pepper, tomatoes with their juice, plenty of seasoning and the stock. Bring to the boil, cover with a lid and cook in a moderate oven (160°C, 325°F, Gas Mark 3) for 1 hour.

Remove from the oven, stir in the soured cream or natural yogurt (the mixture should look streaky) and serve with cooked noodles tossed in a little butter and, if liked, a few poppy or caraway seeds. *Serves 4*

Beef and Parsnip Pie

1 tablespoon oil
1 onion, chopped
2 carrots, chopped
450 g/1 lb minced beef
2 tomatoes, peeled and sliced
salt and freshly ground black pepper
150 ml/¼ pint stock
1 kg/2 lb parsnips
50 g/2 oz butter
2 tablespoons milk
Topping
2 tablespoons fresh white breadcrumbs
25 g/1 oz cheese, grated

Heat the oil in a pan and sauté the onion until softened. Stir in the carrots and beef and cook, stirring, until the beef is lightly browned. Add the tomatoes, seasoning and stock, bring to the boil and simmer for 15 minutes.

Meanwhile peel the parsnips and cook in boiling salted water for 20-25 minutes, until tender. Drain, then mash until smooth. Beat in the butter, milk and a generous amount of black pepper.

Spread half the parsnips in the bottom and up the sides of a greased ovenproof dish. Spoon in the beef mixture and spread the remaining parsnips over the top. Sprinkle the surface with a mixture of the breadcrumbs and cheese and cook in a moderately hot oven (190°C, 375°F, Gas Mark 5) for 30-35 minutes. *Serves 4*

Savoury Beef Bake

450 g/1 lb minced beef
100 g/4 oz beef sausagemeat
1 onion, chopped
2 sticks celery, chopped
50 g/2 oz shredded suet
75 g/3 oz fresh white breadcrumbs
2 tablespoons chopped parsley
2 tablespoons tomato purée
$\frac{1}{4}$ teaspoon dried mixed herbs
salt and freshly ground black pepper
2 hard-boiled eggs
tomato sauce (see page 123)

In a bowl mix together the beef and sausagemeat. Mix in the onion, celery, suet, breadcrumbs, parsley and tomato purée. Add the herbs and season well.

With floured hands, mould the mixture around the hard-boiled eggs, making a loaf shape. Wrap in foil and place in a roasting tin.

Cook in a moderately hot oven (190°C, 375°F, Gas Mark 5) for $1\frac{1}{4}$ hours. Fold back the foil and cook for about a further 15 minutes, until the surface is browned.

Serve, cut in slices, with the tomato sauce. *Serves 4*

Beef Beanpot

1 tablespoon oil
450 g / 1 lb minced beef
2 onions, sliced
2 carrots, sliced
1 stick celery, chopped
1 tablespoon flour
1 (227-g/8-oz) can tomatoes
4 tablespoons red wine
300 ml/$\frac{1}{2}$ pint stock
salt and freshly ground black pepper
1 (432-g/15$\frac{1}{4}$-oz) can red kidney beans
Topping
25 g / 1 oz browned breadcrumbs
50 g / 2 oz Cheddar cheese, grated

Heat the oil in a frying pan and sauté the beef until nicely browned, stirring to break up the lumps. Transfer the beef to an ovenproof dish. Add the onions, carrots and celery to the oil remaining in the pan and sauté for 3-4 minutes. Add to the beef.

Sprinkle the flour into the pan and cook for 1-2 minutes, stirring. Add the tomatoes with their juice and red wine and gradually add the stock. Bring to the boil, stirring, and add the seasoning. Pour into the ovenproof dish. Cover and cook in a moderate oven (180°C, 350°F, Gas Mark 4) for 45 minutes. Add the drained beans and cook for a further 15 minutes.

Remove from the oven and sprinkle the surface with a mixture of the breadcrumbs and cheese. Brown under a hot grill and serve. *Serves 4*

West Country Pie

450 g / 1 lb minced beef
1 medium potato, peeled and cubed
2 carrots, chopped
1 onion, chopped
100 g / 4 oz mushrooms, chopped
salt and freshly ground black pepper
150 ml / $\frac{1}{4}$ pint dry cider
225 g / 8 oz puff pastry
beaten egg to glaze

Mix together the beef, potato, carrots, onion and mushrooms. Season well and place the mixture in a 1-litre/1$\frac{1}{2}$-pint pie dish with a pie funnel placed in the centre. Pour in the cider.

Roll out the pastry and cut away a 2.5-cm/1-inch strip. Dampen the rim of the pie dish, place on the strip of pastry and brush with water. Cover with the pastry lid and flake and flute the edges. Brush with beaten egg and make a hole in the centre for the steam to escape. Decorate the top with leaves made from the pastry trimmings; brush the leaves with egg.

Bake in a hot oven (220°C, 425°F, Gas Mark 7) for 20 minutes. Lower the temperature to moderate (180°C, 350°F, Gas Mark 4) and bake the pie for a further 35-40 minutes, covering the pastry with a piece of foil if it becomes too brown. *Serves 4*

Cheesy Cottage Pie

2 tablespoons oil
2 onions, sliced
450 g / 1 lb minced beef
2 teaspoons flour
50 g / 2 oz mushrooms, sliced
2 tomatoes, peeled and chopped
2 teaspoons Worcestershire sauce
salt and freshly ground black pepper
1 tablespoon tomato purée
150 ml / $\frac{1}{4}$ pint beef stock
350 g / 12 oz cooked potatoes
50 g / 2 oz butter
2 eggs, separated
25 g / 1 oz cheese, grated

Heat the oil in a pan and sauté the onions until softened. Add the beef and cook, stirring to break up the lumps, for about 10 minutes, until browned. Stir in the flour and cook for a further 1-2 minutes. Add the mushrooms, tomatoes, Worcestershire sauce, seasoning, tomato purée and stock. Bring to the boil, cover, lower the heat and simmer for 15 minutes.

Mash the potatoes and beat in the butter with seasoning to taste. Beat in the egg yolks and cheese. Whisk the egg whites until fluffy and fold them into the potato mixture.

Transfer the minced beef mixture to an ovenproof dish and top with the potatoes. Mark the surface with the prongs of a fork and cook in a moderately hot oven (190°C, 375°F, Gas Mark 5) for 35 minutes, until the potatoes are nicely browned. *Serves 4*

Beef and Carrot Pudding

Boiled potatoes sprinkled with plenty of chopped parsley is the only accompaniment needed for this pudding. If you prefer a lighter suet crust, replace 50 g/2 oz of the self-raising flour with the same amount of fresh white breadcrumbs.

2 tablespoons oil
2 onions, chopped
450 g/1 lb minced beef
225 g/8 oz carrots, grated
2 tablespoons tomato purée
1 tablespoon flour
salt and freshly ground black pepper
2 teaspoons Worcestershire sauce
300 ml/½ pint beef stock
225 g/8 oz suet pastry (see Scottish pudding, page 67)

Heat the oil in a pan and sauté the onions until softened. Add the beef and cook, stirring, until browned. Stir in the carrots, tomato purée, flour, seasoning and Worcestershire sauce. Gradually stir in the stock. Bring to the boil and simmer for 5 minutes. Leave to cool.

Meanwhile prepare the pastry and line a 1.25-litre/2-pint greased pudding basin as described in the Scottish pudding recipe on page 67. Spoon in the cooled filling and cover with the pastry lid. Seal the edges and cover with a piece of pleated foil. Steam for 2 hours, remembering to top up the steamer with boiling water from time to time.

To serve, remove the foil and serve from the pudding basin.
Serves 4-6

Texas hash (see page 56); Hungarian minced beef (see page 44)

Beef Scone Pie

2 tablespoons oil
1 onion, sliced
2 carrots, sliced
450 g/1 lb minced beef
1 bay leaf
50 g/2 oz mushrooms, sliced
salt and freshly ground black pepper
300 ml/½ pint beef stock
Topping
200 g/8 oz self-raising flour
pinch of salt
pinch of dried mixed herbs
50 g/2 oz butter or margarine
1 egg
4 tablespoons milk

Heat the oil in a pan and sauté the onion until softened. Stir in the carrots and beef and cook, stirring, until the beef is lightly browned. Add the bay leaf, mushrooms, seasoning and stock. Cover, bring to the boil, then lower the heat and simmer for 20 minutes.

To make the topping, sift the flour and salt into a mixing bowl. Stir in the mixed herbs. Rub in the fat until the mixture resembles fine breadcrumbs. Lightly beat the egg with the milk and add sufficient to mix to a fairly soft dough. Roll out to 3.5-cm/1½-inch thickness and cut into 5-cm/2-inch rounds.

Transfer the beef to an ovenproof casserole, discarding the bay leaf. Arrange the scone rounds in an overlapping circle around the edge of the meat. Brush them with any left-over egg mixture, or milk, and bake in a hot oven (220°C, 425°F, Gas Mark 7) for 10-15 minutes, until the scone topping is well risen and golden brown. *Serves 4*

Lamb patties (see page 61); lamb pasties (see page 60); curried minced lamb (see page 63)

Pancake Layer Pie

If the pancakes and Bolognaise sauce are made in advance and frozen, this dish is a simple assembly job once the pancakes and sauce have thawed, making it a quick main dish.

8 cooked pancakes (see Stuffed pancakes, page 55)
Bolognaise sauce (see page 119)
Topping
1 (142-ml/5-fl oz) carton natural yogurt
1 egg
25 g/1 oz grated Parmesan cheese
Garnish
chopped parsley

Take a round, fairly deep ovenproof dish a little larger than your pancakes and grease it well. Place a pancake in the bottom, spoon over some of the Bolognaise sauce then cover with another pancake. Continue in this way, ending with a layer of sauce.

Mix together the yogurt and egg and spoon over the surface. Sprinkle with grated cheese and cook in a moderate oven (180°C, 350°F, Gas Mark 4) for 30-35 minutes.

Serve garnished with chopped parsley and accompanied by a selection of salads. *Serves 4*

Stuffed Pancakes

Cooked pancakes are good freezer candidates and it's always worthwhile to have some in stock for sweet or savoury dishes. To freeze, pack the cooked, cooled pancakes in piles with greaseproof paper between each one. Wrap in foil, seal and label. Allow to thaw at room temperature before using.

100 g/4 oz plain flour
pinch of salt
1 egg
300 ml/½ pint milk
oil for frying
Filling
Bolognaise sauce (see page 119), made with 4½ tablespoons each of stock and red wine
Topping
25 g/1 oz Parmesan cheese, grated
50 g/2 oz Cheddar cheese, grated

Sift the flour and salt into a bowl. Make a well in the centre and break in the egg. Gradually add the milk, beating the mixture with a wooden spoon to form a smooth batter.

Heat a little oil in a 20-cm/8-inch frying pan and ladle in a little batter to make a thin coating. Cook until the underside is browned. Toss or turn and cook the other side. Turn on to a plate and keep warm while making the other pancakes. This mixture will make about 10 pancakes.

When all the pancakes are made, form each one into a triangle and fill the top pocket of each with some of the hot Bolognaise sauce. Arrange the filled pancakes in a single layer in an ovenproof dish. Sprinkle with the cheeses and pop under a heated grill for 3-4 minutes to melt the cheese. *Serves 4*

Texas Hash

(Illustrated on page 51)

2 tablespoons oil
2 onions, sliced
1 green pepper, seeded and chopped
450 g / 1 lb minced beef
1 (425-g / 15-oz) can tomatoes
75 g / 3 oz long-grain rice
2 teaspoons chilli powder
salt and freshly ground black pepper

Heat the oil in a frying pan and sauté the onions and pepper until softened. Transfer to an ovenproof dish. Add the beef to the frying pan and sauté, stirring to break up the lumps, until browned. Place in the dish with the onions and peppers.

Add the tomatoes with their juice, rice, chilli powder and seasoning. Cover and cook in a moderate oven (180°C, 350°F, Gas Mark 4) for 1¼ hours. *Serves 4*

Family Hot Pot

4 rashers streaky bacon
1 onion, chopped
450 g / 1 lb minced beef
1 (227-g / 8-oz) can tomatoes
2 tablespoons Worcestershire sauce
1 tablespoon tomato purée
pinch of dried mixed herbs
salt and freshly ground black pepper
150 ml / ¼ pint stock or water
450 g / 1 lb potatoes
25 g / 1 oz butter, melted

Remove the bacon rinds, chop the bacon and place in a pan. Cook over a low heat until the fat runs, then add the onion and sauté for 5 minutes. Stir in the beef and sauté until evenly browned. Add the tomatoes with their juice, Worcestershire sauce, tomato purée, herbs, seasoning and stock. Bring to the boil, reduce the heat, then cover and simmer for 20 minutes.

Peel and thinly slice the potatoes.

Spoon half the meat mixture into an ovenproof dish and cover with half the potato slices. Sprinkle with salt. Spoon in the remaining meat mixture and cover with the rest of the potato slices, overlapping. Sprinkle with a little more salt and brush the potatoes with melted butter.

Cook, uncovered, in a moderate oven (180°C, 350°F, Gas Mark 4) for about 1 hour.

Serve with a green vegetable. *Serves 4*

Stuffed Marrow

2 rashers bacon
1 onion, chopped
350 g/12 oz minced beef
50 g/2 oz cooked long-grain rice
salt and freshly ground black pepper
1 egg, lightly beaten
1 medium marrow
Cheesy Mustard Sauce
25 g/1 oz butter
25 g/1 oz flour
1 teaspoon dry mustard
salt and freshly ground white pepper
150 ml/$\frac{1}{4}$ pint milk
100 g/4 oz cheese, grated
1 teaspoon vinegar

Remove the bacon rinds and chop the bacon. Place in a frying pan and cook over a moderate heat until the fat runs. Add the onion and sauté until softened. Add the beef and cook until browned. Drain off the excess fat and stir in the cooked rice with plenty of seasoning. Bind the mixture together with the lightly beaten egg.

Wipe the marrow and slice off one end. Using a tablespoon, scoop out the seeds. Fill the cavity with the prepared stuffing and wrap the marrow in a piece of lightly oiled foil. Place in a roasting tin and cook in a moderate oven (180°C, 350°F, Gas Mark 4) for 45 minutes-1 hour.

To make the sauce, melt the butter in a pan and stir in the flour, mustard and seasoning. Cook for 1-2 minutes. Gradually add the milk, stirring, and cook until thickened. Finally, stir in the cheese and vinegar and simmer for about 1 minute.

Serve the marrow, cut in thick slices, with the cheesy mustard sauce poured over. *Serves 4*

Bean-stuffed Peppers

These make a good snack meal and I find they are popular with children.

4 green peppers
2 tablespoons oil
1 onion, chopped
350 g/12 oz minced beef
50 g/2 oz mushrooms, chopped
1 (447-g/15¾-oz) can baked beans
2 tablespoons tomato purée
salt and freshly ground black pepper
½ teaspoon dried basil

Slice the tops off the peppers and take out the cores and seeds. Trim the bases if necessary so that the peppers stand upright. Blanch the peppers in boiling salted water for 3 minutes. Drain and refresh with cold water then leave upside down to drain while preparing the filling.

Heat the oil in a frying pan and sauté the onion for 3 minutes. Add the beef and sauté for about 10 minutes, until lightly browned. Add the mushrooms, baked beans, tomato purée, seasoning and basil and bring the mixture to the boil.

Stand the peppers upright in an ovenproof dish and fill with the meat mixture. Cover with a piece of foil and cook in a moderately hot oven (190°C, 375°F, Gas Mark 5) for about 40 minutes.

Serve with rice or noodles. *Serves 4*

Lamb Pasties

(Illustrated on page 52)

225 g/8 oz minced lamb
4 spring onions, chopped
1 carrot, grated
pinch of dried rosemary
salt and freshly ground black pepper
Pastry
225 g/8 oz plain flour
$\frac{1}{4}$ teaspoon salt
110 g/4 oz lard
about 3 tablespoons water
beaten egg to glaze

Mix together the lamb, onions, carrot and rosemary with plenty of seasoning.

To make the pastry, sift the flour and salt into a mixing bowl. Rub in the lard until the mixture resembles fine breadcrumbs. Add the water and mix to a firm dough. Wrap in cling film and chill for 30 minutes.

Roll out the dough on a lightly floured surface and cut into four 18-cm/7-inch circles. Divide the filling between the circles, placing it in the centre of each. Dampen the edges and bring them together at the top to form a pasty. Press the edges together well and crimp them. Place the pasties on a greased baking sheet and brush with lightly beaten egg.

Bake in a hot oven (220°C, 425°F, Gas Mark 7) for 15 minutes. Lower the temperature to moderate (180°C, 350°F, Gas Mark 4) and bake for a further 15-20 minutes, until nicely browned. Serve hot or cold. *Serves 4*

Lamb Patties

(Illustrated on page 52)

6 slices white bread
3 tablespoons milk
3 tablespoons oil
1 onion, chopped
1 clove garlic, crushed
575 g/1¼ lb minced lamb
2 tablespoons chopped parsley
pinch of dried rosemary
salt and freshly ground black pepper
1 egg, lightly beaten
12 rashers streaky bacon
50 g/2 oz butter

With a 5-cm/2-inch cutter, cut out 12 rounds from the slices of bread. Discarding the crusts, break up the trimmings and place in a bowl. Pour on the milk and leave to soak.

Heat 1 tablespoon of the oil in a frying pan and sauté the onion and garlic for about 10 minutes, until softened and a golden brown colour.

In a bowl mix together the lamb, parsley, rosemary and cooked onion. Season well and bind with the lightly beaten egg and soaked bread.

Remove the bacon rinds, discard any pieces of bone and stretch the rashers until thin, with the blade of a knife.

With floured hands, divide the lamb mixture in 12 equal-sized portions. Shape each portion into a ball, then flatten and shape into a cake 5 cm/2 inches in diameter. Wrap a bacon rasher around each patty and secure with a piece of thread or a wooden cocktail stick.

Heat the remaining oil in a large frying pan and fry the patties over a low heat for about 15 minutes on each side.

Meanwhile heat the butter in a separate pan and fry the bread circles for 2-3 minutes on each side, until crisp and brown.

To serve, arrange the bread croûtes on a serving dish. Remove the thread or cocktail sticks from the patties and place each one on a croûte. *Serves 6*

Lamb-stuffed Aubergines

2 large aubergines
25 g / 1 oz butter
1 onion, chopped
2 rashers streaky bacon, chopped
175 g / 6 oz minced lamb
1 clove garlic, crushed
1 (425-g / 15-oz) can tomatoes
1 tablespoon tomato purée
pinch of dried oregano
salt and freshly ground black pepper
100 g / 4 oz cheese, grated

Slice the aubergines in half lengthwise. Using a grapefruit knife, carefully remove the flesh and chop coarsely. Place on a plate, sprinkle with salt and leave for 30 minutes. Blanch the aubergine shells in boiling salted water for 5 minutes. Drain and refresh in cold water.

Melt the butter in a frying pan and sauté the onion and bacon for 5 minutes. Stir in the lamb and sauté until evenly browned. Add the garlic, tomatoes with their juice, tomato purée, oregano and seasoning. Bring to the boil and simmer for 10 minutes.

Place the aubergine flesh in a sieve and rinse in cold water. Drain well and add to the lamb mixture. Allow the filling to simmer, uncovered, for a further 5 minutes to reduce and thicken.

Place the aubergine shells in a fairly shallow ovenproof dish and pile in the filling. Sprinkle with grated cheese and cook in a moderate oven (180°C, 350°F, Gas Mark 4) for about 30 minutes. Serve hot accompanied by a tossed green salad. *Serves 4*

Curried Minced Lamb

(Illustrated on page 52)

1 tablespoon oil
2 onions, sliced
2 cloves garlic, crushed
1 tablespoon curry powder
675 g/1½ lb minced lamb
½ teaspoon ground turmeric
pinch each of ground ginger, paprika and cayenne
salt and freshly ground black pepper
1 (283-ml/10-fl oz) carton natural yogurt

Heat the oil in a flameproof casserole and sauté the onions and garlic until softened. Stir in the curry powder and cook, stirring, for 2-3 minutes. Add the lamb and cook, stirring, until browned. Add the spices and seasoning and stir in the yogurt. Cover and simmer for about 1 hour.

Serve with rice and a selection of traditional curry side dishes – tomato and onion slices, salted peanuts, chutney and banana slices sprinkled with lemon juice. *Serves 6*

Pork Pasties

225 g/8 oz minced pork
1 onion, grated
1 carrot, grated
1 cooking apple, peeled, cored and chopped
2 teaspoons chopped fresh sage
salt and freshly ground black pepper
Pastry
225 g/8 oz plain flour
$\frac{1}{4}$ teaspoon salt
85 g/3 oz margarine
25 g/1 oz lard
about 3 tablespoons water
beaten egg to glaze

Mix together the pork, onion, carrot, apple and sage with plenty of seasoning.

To make the pastry, sift the flour and salt into a mixing bowl. Rub in the fats until the mixture resembles breadcrumbs. Add the water and mix to a firm dough. Wrap in cling film and chill for 30 minutes.

Take two-thirds of the dough and roll it out on a lightly floured surface. Cut into four 10-cm/4-inch circles and use to line four patty tins of the same diameter, pressing the dough in well. Divide the pork filling between the lined tins. Roll out the remaining dough and cut out four more circles for the lids. Dampen the edges and press the lids over the filling. Flute the edges together and brush the surfaces with lightly beaten egg. Decorate with leaves made from the pastry trimmings and brush with egg.

Bake in a hot oven (220°C, 425°F, Gas Mark 7) for 15 minutes. Lower the temperature to moderate (180°C, 350°F, Gas Mark 4) and bake for a further 25-30 minutes, until the pasties are nicely browned. Serve hot. *Serves 4*

Variation

Beef Pasties Replace the minced pork with minced beef. In place of the apple and sage use 1 tablespoon bottled horse-radish sauce and 1 tablespoon chopped parsley.

Pork Roll en Croûte

450 g/1 lb minced pork
1 onion, chopped
1 clove garlic, crushed
2 teaspoons chopped fresh sage
100 g/4 oz mushrooms, chopped
2 tablespoons chopped parsley
salt and freshly ground black pepper
1 teaspoon Worcestershire sauce
2 eggs, lightly beaten
350 g/12 oz puff pastry

Place the pork, onion, garlic, sage, mushrooms, parsley and seasoning in a bowl. Add the Worcestershire sauce and sufficient egg to bind the mixture.

Roll out the pastry to a rectangle approximately 30 by 25 cm/12 by 10 inches. Form the pork mixture into a large, fat sausage shape and place it down the centre of the pastry.

Brush the pastry edges with water and fold over the sides and ends to enclose the filling. Press the edges together to seal and place the roll, seam-side down, on a lightly greased baking sheet.

Brush the pastry with the remaining beaten egg and decorate with leaves made from the pastry trimmings; brush the leaves with egg. Make two slits in the top and bake in a hot oven (220°C, 425°F, Gas Mark 7) for 15 minutes. Lower the temperature to moderately hot (190°C, 375°F, Gas Mark 5) and bake for a further 40-45 minutes, covering the pastry with foil to prevent it becoming too brown.

Slice and serve hot. *Serves 4*

Home-made Sausages

These are a far cry from the commercially-produced, so-called sausages of today. It's not necessary to encase the mixture in skin nor is any special equipment needed, apart from a mincer or food processor. The meat can be minced finely or coarsely according to your preference.

225 g/8 oz minced pork
225 g/8 oz minced veal
50 g/2 oz streaky bacon, minced
50 g/2 oz shredded suet
100 g/4 oz fresh white breadcrumbs
salt and freshly ground black pepper
2 tablespoons chopped parsley
pinch of ground nutmeg
2 teaspoons chopped fresh sage
grated rind of 1 lemon
oil for shallow frying

Mix together the pork, veal, bacon, suet and breadcrumbs. Season generously and mix in the parsley, nutmeg, sage and lemon rind.

With floured hands, form the mixture into sausage shapes or round, flat cakes.

Shallow fry in a little oil and serve, as a breakfast or brunch treat, with fried eggs, mushrooms, tomatoes and fried bread.
Serves 4-6

Scottish Pudding

This savoury suet pudding makes good cold weather fare and is delicious served with jacket potatoes and turnips mashed with plenty of butter and seasoning.

225 g/8 oz minced lamb
225 g/8 oz minced pork
2 onions, grated
100 g/4 oz shredded suet
100 g/4 oz fine oatmeal
grated rind of 1 lemon
100 g/4 oz mushrooms, chopped
2 tablespoons chopped parsley
salt and freshly ground black pepper
4 tablespoons stock or red wine
Suet Pastry
225 g/8 oz self-raising flour
$\frac{1}{2}$ teaspoon salt
110 g/4 oz shredded suet
150 ml/$\frac{1}{4}$ pint water

Mix together the lamb, pork, onion, suet, oatmeal, lemon rind, mushrooms and parsley with plenty of seasoning. Moisten with the stock or red wine.

To make the pastry, sift the flour and salt into a mixing bowl and mix in the shredded suet. Pour in the water and, using a round-bladed knife, mix to a light, elastic dough. Turn the dough on to a floured surface and knead lightly. Roll out to a circle large enough to line the base and sides of a 1.25-litre/2-pint pudding basin. Cut away one-quarter of the dough (it will be a triangular shape) and keep it aside for the lid. Line the greased pudding basin with the dough, securing the two edges with water.

Spoon the filling into the lined basin. Roll out the reserved piece of dough to make a lid. Dampen the outer edges and place it over the filling, pressing the two edges together.

Cover the top with a piece of foil with a pleat in the centre. Secure the foil with string. Steam the pudding for $2\frac{1}{4}$ hours, topping up the steamer with boiling water from time to time.

To serve, remove the foil and turn the pudding on to a heated serving dish or serve from the basin. *Serves 4-6*

Veal Roll

50 g / 2 oz butter
1 onion, chopped
450 g / 1 lb minced veal
100 g / 4 oz pork sausagemeat
2 teaspoons chopped fresh thyme
1 tablespoon chopped parsley
grated rind of 1 lemon
salt and freshly ground black pepper
Pastry
350 g / 12 oz plain flour
$\frac{1}{2}$ teaspoon salt
85 g / 3 oz margarine
85 g / 3 oz lard
about 4 tablespoons water
beaten egg to glaze

Heat the butter in a frying pan and sauté the onion until softened. Add the veal and sausagemeat and cook, stirring, for 5 minutes. Mix in the herbs, lemon rind and seasoning. Leave to cool.

To make the pastry, sift the flour and salt into a mixing bowl. Rub in the fats until the mixture resembles breadcrumbs. Add the water and mix to a firm dough. Wrap in cling film and chill for 30 minutes.

Roll the dough out on a lightly floured surface to an oblong about 30 by 25 cm / 12 by 10 inches. Trim the edges. Place the filling in the centre, dampen the pastry edges and bring them over the filling. Press together to seal along the top and ends. Place the roll on a greased baking sheet, seam-side down, and brush with beaten egg. Make some leaves from the pastry trimmings and place on the roll; brush with beaten egg.

Bake in a hot oven (220°C, 425°F, Gas Mark 7) for 10 minutes. Lower the temperature to moderate (160°C, 325°F, Gas Mark 3) and bake for about a further $1\frac{1}{4}$ hours, covering the pastry with a piece of foil to prevent it becoming too brown. *Serves 6*

Picnic Pie

350 g / 12 oz minced veal
450 g / 1 lb minced pork
1 onion, grated
¼ teaspoon dried sage
grated rind of 1 lemon
2 tablespoons chopped parsley
salt and freshly ground black pepper
Hot Water Crust Pastry
350 g / 12 oz plain flour
½ teaspoon salt
110 g / 4 oz lard
150 ml / ¼ pint water
1 egg yolk
beaten egg to glaze

Mix together the veal, pork and onion. Stir in the sage, lemon rind, parsley and plenty of seasoning.

To make the pastry, sift the flour and salt into a mixing bowl. Put the lard and water in a small saucepan and place over a low heat to melt the fat, then bring to the boil. Make a well in the centre of the flour and add the egg yolk, cover with a little of the flour then pour in the lard mixture. Mix quickly with a wooden spoon to form a soft dough. Turn on to a floured board and knead until pliable. Roll out three-quarters of the dough (keeping the remainder warm under the upturned bowl) and use to line the base and sides of a 20-cm / 8-inch well-greased loose-bottomed cake tin. Press in the meat mixture. Roll out the remaining dough for a lid. Brush the edges with water and press over the filling. Press the two edges together, trim and crimp. Make some leaves from the pastry trimmings. Brush the top with beaten egg, put the leaves in position and glaze them with egg. Make a hole in the centre, stand the pie on a baking sheet and bake in a moderately hot oven (200°C, 400°F, Gas Mark 6) for 30 minutes. Lower the oven to moderate (160°C, 325°F, Gas Mark 3) and bake for a further 1¼-1½ hours, covering the pie with foil to prevent it becoming too brown.

Leave the pie to cool, then remove it from the tin. When it is almost cold, pour in some jellied stock made by dissolving 2 teaspoons gelatine in 300 ml / ½ pint stock. Leave to set and serve cold. *Serves 6-8*

5
Around the World

Most countries have their own traditional minced meat specialities, many of which are recognised as classic dishes.

Some dishes which originated in one country have been adopted and absorbed into the cuisine of other countries – moussaka for example was originally a Rumanian dish but has found its way into the cuisine of the Eastern Mediterranean countries.

Today our culinary horizons have been broadened through travel and the choice of restaurants specialising in different cuisines; many so-called 'foreign' dishes are no longer alien to us. It's also now very easy for the cook to obtain a wide variety of specialist ingredients to produce the authentic dishes from other countries at home.

I've endeavoured to make the recipes in this chapter as authentic as possible and hope that when you try them in your own kitchen the dish will bring back holiday memories or remind you of a dish you may have enjoyed in a restaurant.

Albondigas

These meatballs originate from South America, but are also popular in Spain and Portugal.

2 tablespoons fresh white breadcrumbs
2 tablespoons milk
450 g / 1 lb minced beef
1 onion, grated
pinch of cayenne
salt and freshly ground black pepper
flour for coating
1 tablespoon oil
50 g / 2 oz butter
Sauce
2 tablespoons oil
1 onion, chopped
450 g / 1 lb tomatoes, peeled and sliced
$\frac{1}{4}$ teaspoon dried thyme
salt and freshly ground black pepper
300 ml / $\frac{1}{2}$ pint stock
pinch of sugar

Soak the breadcrumbs in the milk. In a bowl mix together the beef, onion, seasonings and soaked breadcrumbs. With floured hands, shape the mixture into walnut-sized balls and toss lightly in flour.

Heat the oil and butter in a frying pan and cook the meatballs over a low heat for about 15 minutes, until nicely browned and cooked through. Keep warm.

Meanwhile make the sauce. Heat the oil in a pan and sauté the onion until softened. Add the tomatoes, thyme and seasoning and simmer for about 10 minutes, until reduced to a thick sauce. Stir in the stock, add the sugar and simmer for a further 10-15 minutes.

Place the meatballs in a serving dish and pour over the sauce. Serve with rice. *Serves 4*

Steak Tartare

For this classic dish of raw steak (yes, raw) it is essential to use either freshly, finely minced fillet or rump steak. It can be served surrounded by mounds of diced raw vegetables – onions and green and red peppers – and finely chopped gherkins and capers.

450 g / 1 lb fillet or rump steak
3 egg yolks
4 tablespoons oil
2 tablespoons chopped parsley
salt and freshly ground black pepper
Garnish
crisp lettuce leaves
grated horseradish (optional)

Trim and mince the steak finely. Mix in the egg yolks, oil, parsley and seasoning. Divide the mixture into four and shape each portion into a round, flat cake.

Arrange on a bed of crisp lettuce leaves and if liked, add a sprinkling of grated horseradish.

Jacket potatoes or potato crisps go well with steak tartare.
Serves 4

Chilli con Carne

This is a Mexican speciality and is an ideal dish to serve for a winter's supper party. I usually serve it in individual bowls with a spoon rather than a fork. Crusty French bread and a tossed green or mixed salad make perfect accompaniments.

1 tablespoon oil
2 onions, sliced
1 clove garlic, crushed
450 g / 1 lb minced beef
2 (425-g / 15-oz) cans tomatoes
2 teaspoons chilli powder
$\frac{1}{2}$ teaspoon cumin
1 tablespoon tomato purée
150 ml / $\frac{1}{4}$ pint red wine
salt and freshly ground black pepper
1 bay leaf
1 (432-g / 15$\frac{1}{4}$-oz) can red kidney beans

Heat the oil in a heavy-based saucepan and sauté the onions and garlic until softened. Add the beef and cook until browned, stirring to break up the lumps. Add the tomatoes with their juice. Bring to the boil, cover and simmer over a low heat for about 45 minutes, stirring occasionally – it may be necessary to add a little boiling water if the liquid evaporates.

In a small bowl, blend the chilli powder with a little of the hot liquid from the beef. Stir this into the beef together with the cumin and tomato purée. Add the red wine, seasoning, bay leaf and drained beans. Cover and simmer for a further 1 hour. Discard the bay leaf and serve. *Serves 4*

Bobotie

Bobotie (pronounced boh-boo-tee) hails from South Africa and is a spicy, slightly curried mixture with fruit and nuts. It's good served with saffron rice, to which you can add some raisins 5 minutes before the end of the cooking time, and a side dish of mango chutney. Like so many minced dishes it makes an ideal choice for a buffet party.

25 g/1 oz butter
2 onions, chopped
1 dessert apple, peeled and chopped
2 teaspoons curry powder
450 g/1 lb minced beef
25 g/1 oz fresh white breadcrumbs
2 eggs
1 tablespoon mango chutney
1 tablespoon flaked almonds
1 teaspoon sultanas
salt and freshly ground black pepper
4 bay leaves
150 ml/¼ pint milk

Heat the butter in a frying pan and sauté the onions and apple for about 10 minutes, until softened. Stir in the curry powder and cook for 1-2 minutes.

In a bowl, mix together the minced beef, breadcrumbs, one of the eggs, the chutney, almonds and sultanas. Stir in the onion and apple and season well.

Spread the mixture in a lightly greased ovenproof dish, arrange the bay leaves on top and cook, uncovered, in a moderate oven (180°C, 350°F, Gas Mark 4) for 30 minutes.

Lightly whisk together the remaining egg and the milk. Take the dish from the oven and remove any excess fat from the surface by drawing absorbent paper across the top. Pour over the egg and milk and cook the dish for a further 30-35 minutes, until the top is lightly browned. *Serves 4*

Lasagne Verdi

This well-known Italian dish is a bit of a fiddle to make, but to compensate for this the preparation and assembling can be done in advance, making lasagne a good fork supper or party dish.

12 sheets lasagne verdi
Bolognaise sauce (see page 119)
Béchamel Sauce
600 ml / 1 pint milk
1 bay leaf
4-6 white peppercorns
freshly grated nutmeg
few slices onion
40 g / 1½ oz butter
40 g / 1½ oz flour
Topping
50 g / 2 oz cheese, grated
2 tablespoons grated Parmesan cheese

Cook the lasagne in boiling salted water with 1 tablespoon oil added – according to the directions on the packet. Drain it in a colander and rinse in cold water. Lay the sheets of lasagne on absorbent paper to dry.

Meanwhile make the Bolognaise sauce (see page 119) and béchamel sauce.

To make the béchamel sauce, place the milk, bay leaf, peppercorns, nutmeg and onion in a pan. Bring slowly just to the boil. Pour into a jug and leave to cool. Melt the butter in a clean pan and stir in the flour. Cook for 1 minute. Gradually strain in the infused milk, stirring to make a smooth sauce. Bring to the boil and cook, stirring, for 1-2 minutes.

To assemble the lasagne, line the base of a lightly oiled ovenproof dish with some of the lasagne. Spread with a layer of Bolognaise sauce followed by a layer of béchamel sauce. Continue in this way ending up with a layer of béchamel sauce. Sprinkle the surface with a mixture of the cheeses and cook in a moderately hot oven (200°C, 400°F, Gas Mark 6) for 40-45 minutes, until browned and bubbling. Or cool, cover with cling film and store in the refrigerator until ready to cook. Serve with a tossed green salad. *Serves 4*

Beef Kofta

In order to achieve the authentic flavour of this Indian dish it is essential to make up your own mixture of spices (garam masala) and to use coconut milk made by grating the white flesh from a coconut and pouring over 150 ml/¼ pint boiling water. Leave to stand for 30 minutes, then strain off the liquid and make it up to 600 ml/1 pint with cold water. Ghee is equivalent to clarified butter and can be bought in cans.

450 g/1 lb minced beef
3 fresh chillies, finely chopped
1 onion, grated
2 cloves garlic, crushed
salt and freshly ground black pepper
1 egg, lightly beaten
4 tablespoons ghee
2 onions, sliced
2 tablespoons garam masala (see note)
2 teaspoons paprika
600 ml/1 pint coconut milk
2 teaspoons lemon juice

Mix together the beef, chillies, grated onion, garlic and seasoning. Add sufficient beaten egg to bind and, with floured hands, shape the mixture into walnut-sized balls.

Heat half the ghee in a pan and sauté the meatballs until brown on all sides. Remove and drain on absorbent paper.

Add the remaining ghee to the pan and heat. Sauté the onions until softened. Add the garam masala and paprika and cook, stirring all the time, for 5 minutes. Gradually stir in the coconut milk. Add the meatballs, cover the pan and simmer for 30 minutes, shaking the pan from time to time. Sharpen the sauce with lemon juice and serve the kofta with rice and side dishes. *Serves 4*

Note To make garam masala grind together (in a coffee grinder or pestle and mortar) 50 g/2 oz each of coriander seeds, black peppercorns and cumin seeds with 4 teaspoons cloves and 15 g/½ oz cardamom seeds. Mix in 3-4 teaspoons ground cinnamon. Store (for up to 4 weeks) in an airtight container.

Dolmas

This traditional dish from Turkey, served as a main course, is a minced lamb mixture wrapped in vine leaves. You can buy canned vine leaves in specialist stores, but young cabbage leaves make a good substitute.

2 tablespoons oil
1 onion, chopped
100 g/4 oz long-grain rice
900 ml/1½ pints stock (see note) or water
450 g/1 lb minced lamb
2 tablespoons chopped parsley
2 teaspoons chopped fresh mint
2 teaspoons chopped fresh dill
salt and freshly ground black pepper
12 young cabbage leaves
1 (142-ml/5-fl oz) carton natural yogurt

Heat the oil in a frying pan and sauté the onion until transparent. Stir in the rice and cook, stirring, until lightly coloured. Add sufficient stock to cover the rice and cook over a low heat, stirring, until the rice is tender and the liquid is completely absorbed.

When the rice mixture is cool, mix in the lamb, parsley, mint, dill and seasoning.

Cook the cabbage leaves in boiling salted water for 2 minutes. Drain and cut out the coarse centre stalk.

Spread the leaves out on a board and place a spoonful of the lamb mixture in the centre of each one. Fold the edges over the filling to make small, neat parcels. Arrange the parcels, with the folds underneath, in a single layer in a shallow pan. Pour in sufficient stock just to cover the dolmas. Now cover with foil, pressing it close to the surface to keep the dolmas under the stock. Cook over a low heat for about 1 hour.

With a draining spoon, lift the dolmas from the stock on to a serving dish. Serve the yogurt separately. *Serves 4-6*

Note You really need a stock made from veal or lamb bones. Do not use a beef stock as this is too strong. A stock made from a commercially-prepared chicken or herb stock cube can be used, but use only one cube to 900 ml/1½ pints water.

Greek Keftedes

These you will find served throughout Greece and in many Greek restaurants here.

2 eggs
50 g / 2 oz fresh white breadcrumbs
1 onion, grated
2 teaspoons chopped fresh mint
2 tablespoons chopped parsley
1 tablespoon wine vinegar or lemon juice
salt and freshly ground black pepper
1 kg / 2 lb minced lamb
flour for coating
oil for shallow frying
tomato sauce (see page 123)

Break the eggs into a large mixing bowl and beat lightly with a fork. Stir in the breadcrumbs, onion, mint, parsley, wine vinegar and seasoning. Leave to stand for 15 minutes.

Add the minced lamb to the mixture in the bowl, and using your hands, mix all the ingredients thoroughly. With floured hands, shape the mixture into balls, about the size of an egg. Roll lightly in flour and flatten into patty shapes.

Heat the oil in a frying pan and fry the keftedes for about 5 minutes on each side, until lightly browned and cooked through. Drain on absorbent paper and serve with tomato sauce. *Serves 6*

Moussaka

This is a dish of Rumanian origin, traditionally made with minced lamb, which is now eaten throughout the Eastern Mediterranean countries. If you want to sample another version try the recipe on page 111 which has a sauce topping.

3 medium aubergines
salt
4 tablespoons oil
1 large onion, sliced
675 g/1½ lb minced lamb
4 tomatoes, peeled and sliced
1 clove garlic, crushed
1 teaspoon paprika
freshly ground black pepper
2 tablespoons tomato purée
pinch of dried oregano
150 ml/¼ pint stock
Topping
1 (142-ml/5-fl oz) carton natural yogurt
2 egg yolks
1 tablespoon flour

Slice the aubergines and place in a single layer on a large plate. Sprinkle with salt and leave for 1 hour.

Heat half the oil in a pan and sauté the onion for about 5 minutes, until softened. Add the lamb and sauté, stirring the mixture, until the lamb is browned. Add the tomatoes, garlic, paprika, black pepper, tomato purée, oregano and stock. Bring to the boil, cover the pan and simmer for 30 minutes.

Meanwhile rinse the aubergine slices in cold water and pat dry with absorbent paper. Heat the remaining oil in a frying pan and fry the aubergine slices, a few at a time, until lightly browned on both sides. Drain on absorbent paper.

Arrange alternate layers of aubergine slices and the lamb mixture in an oiled ovenproof dish, beginning and ending with a layer of aubergine.

Mix together the yogurt, egg yolks and flour and spoon over the aubergines. Cook in a moderate oven (180°C, 350°F, Gas Mark 4) for about 40 minutes until bubbling hot and nicely browned. *Serves 6*

Turkish Kebabs

(Illustrated on page 86)

For these kebabs the meat mixture is shaped into long rolls about the size of sausages. The secret of success is to make the mixture fine and smooth. Serve them with rice, natural yogurt and a tomato and onion salad sprinkled with chopped fresh herbs.

675 g/1½ lb minced lamb
1 onion, chopped
1 clove garlic, crushed
2 teaspoons ground cumin
salt and freshly ground black pepper
pinch of cayenne
2 tablespoons chopped parsley
oil

Pass the lamb, onion and garlic through the mincer twice, to form a smooth mixture. Stir in the cumin, seasonings and parsley and mix well together.

With floured hands, shape the mixture into sausages about 6 cm/2½ inches long. Place in a single layer on a plate, cover with cling film and leave to chill in the refrigerator for several hours.

To cook, thread the kebabs on to oiled skewers and brush them all over with oil. Cook under a preheated moderately hot grill for 10-15 minutes, turning the kebabs during cooking. *Serves 4*

Meatballs in Egg and Lemon Sauce

This is a traditional Greek dish.

2 slices white bread
675 g/1½ lb minced lamb
2 tablespoons chopped parsley
1 onion, grated
1 clove garlic, crushed
salt and freshly ground black pepper
Egg and Lemon Sauce
3 egg yolks
juice of 1 lemon
150 ml/¼ pint chicken stock or water
salt and freshly ground white pepper
Garnish
chopped parsley

Soak the bread in water, squeeze dry and crumble. Mix together the bread, lamb, parsley, onion, garlic and seasoning. With floured hands, shape the mixture into walnut-sized balls.

Simmer the meatballs in lightly salted water for 30 minutes.

To make the sauce, place the egg yolks in a basin over a pan of simmering water and whisk until lighter in colour and thickened. Gradually whisk in the lemon juice, stock and seasoning.

Drain the meatballs and pile in a heated serving dish. Pour over the egg and lemon sauce, garnish with chopped parsley and serve. *Serves 4*

Caribbean Lamb

1 tablespoon oil
50 g / 2 oz butter
2 onions, sliced
675 g / 1½ lb minced lamb
1 tablespoon curry powder
½ teaspoon turmeric
pinch each of ground ginger and cayenne
salt and freshly ground black pepper
2 tomatoes, peeled and chopped
2 teaspoons lemon juice
300 ml / ½ pint light stock or water

Heat the oil and butter together in a flameproof casserole and sauté the onions until softened. Stir in the lamb and sauté until browned. Add the spices, seasoning, tomatoes, lemon juice and stock (the liquid should just cover the meat).

Cover and simmer very gently for about 40 minutes, until the meat is cooked and the sauce reduced.

Serve with boiled rice, sliced bananas tossed in lemon juice and a selection of chutneys. *Serves 4-6*

Samosas

(Illustrated on page 85)

These are deep fried snacks which are eaten throughout India. Originally the pastry parcel contained meat at one end and something sweet at the other, rather like our original Cornish pasty which was a convenient way of carrying a packed lunch. The most popular filling is a mixture of minced lamb, potatoes and peas.

1 tablespoon oil
1 clove garlic, crushed
175 g/6 oz minced lamb
1 potato, grated
50 g/2 oz peas
$\frac{1}{4}$ teaspoon turmeric
$\frac{1}{2}$ teaspoon garam masala (optional, see page 76)
salt and freshly ground black pepper
oil for deep frying
Pastry
200 g/8 oz plain flour
$\frac{1}{2}$ teaspoon salt
100 g/4 oz margarine
$4\frac{1}{2}$ tablespoons milk

Heat the oil in a frying pan and sauté the garlic and lamb until browned on all sides. Stir in the potato, peas, turmeric and garam masala and cook, stirring to prevent the mixture from sticking, for about 5 minutes. Season and leave to cool while making the pastry.

To make the pastry, sift the flour and salt into a bowl and rub in the margarine until the mixture resembles fine breadcrumbs. Mix in the milk to form a tacky dough. With floured hands, break off balls the size of walnuts and roll each one out on a well-floured board to make a thin circle. (The mixture makes about 25.)

In the centre of each circle place a good teaspoon of the filling. Dampen the edges and fold them over to make a triangular-shaped patty completely enclosing the filling.

Heat the oil and fry the samosas, a few at a time, until golden brown. Drain on absorbent paper and serve either hot or cold, but they are nicer hot. *Makes about 25*

Veal-stuffed Cannelloni

Here's another popular Italian speciality. If you can't obtain veal easily, use either minced lamb or beef. All it needs to accompany it is a salad, and the Chianti of course!

8 cannelloni tubes
Filling
50 g/2 oz butter
50 g/2 oz mushrooms, chopped
350 g/12 oz minced veal
pinch of nutmeg
salt and freshly ground black pepper
600 ml/1 pint tomato sauce (see page 123)
Topping
grated Parmesan cheese
25 g/1 oz butter

Cook the cannelloni in boiling salted water, with 1 tablespoon oil added, according to the directions on the packet. Drain and rinse in cold water.

To make the filling, heat the butter in a frying pan and sauté the mushrooms for 3-4 minutes. Stir in the minced veal, nutmeg and seasoning and brown the veal. Add about 6 tablespoons water and allow the mixture to simmer for about 20 minutes, stirring occasionally. Allow to cool slightly, then fill the cannelloni – the easiest way to do this is to spoon the filling into a large piping bag fitted with a plain tube and pipe it into the cannelloni. Even so, careful handling is necessary to avoid the cannelloni splitting.

Arrange the filled cannelloni in a greased ovenproof dish and pour over the tomato sauce. Sprinkle the surface generously with grated Parmesan cheese and dot with butter. Cook, uncovered, in a moderate oven (180°C, 350°F, Gas Mark 4) for 30-35 minutes, until bubbling and lightly browned.
Serves 4

Samosas (see page 83)

Hungarian Veal

2 tablespoons oil
2 onions, sliced
2 cloves garlic, crushed
900 g/2 lb minced veal
2 tablespoons paprika
¼ teaspoon caraway seeds
1 bay leaf
pinch each of dried marjoram and thyme
salt and freshly ground black pepper
225 g/8 oz button mushrooms, sliced
1 (425-g/15-oz) can tomatoes
1 green pepper, seeded and chopped
1 red pepper, seeded and chopped
1 (142-ml/5-fl oz) carton soured cream

Heat the oil in a flameproof casserole and sauté the onions and garlic for 5 minutes. Stir in the veal and sauté until browned. Add the paprika, caraway seeds, herbs and seasoning and simmer for 5 minutes.

Add the mushrooms, tomatoes and peppers. Cover and cook in a moderate oven (160°C, 325°F, Gas Mark 3) for 1¾-2 hours.

Just before serving, discard the bay leaf, stir in the soured cream (the mixture should look streaky) and serve with noodles mixed with a few poppy seeds. *Serves 6-8*

Turkish kebabs (see page 80); barbecue sauce (see page 121)

Frikadeller

These spicy meatballs are popular in Denmark and can be served hot with a tomato sauce or cold, cut into slices and used as a topping, together with various garnishes, for open sandwiches. Served hot, they are good with red cabbage.

2 slices white bread
1 tablespoon milk
225 g/8 oz minced veal
225 g/8 oz minced pork
1 small onion, grated
2 teaspoons chopped parsley
salt and freshly ground black pepper
$\frac{1}{2}$ teaspoon allspice
1 egg, lightly beaten
flour for coating
1 tablespoon oil
50 g/2 oz butter
Garnish
chopped parsley

Cut the crusts from the bread, then soak the bread in the milk. Squeeze dry and mix with the veal and pork. Mix in the onion, parsley, plenty of seasoning and the allspice. Bind the mixture with the lightly beaten egg. With floured hands, shape the mixture into about 10 small oblongs and lightly coat in flour.

Heat the oil and butter in a frying pan and fry the frikadeller for about 15 minutes, until browned on both sides and cooked through.

Serve sprinkled with chopped parsley. *Serves 4*

Chinese Pork Balls

450 g/1 lb minced pork
1 clove garlic, crushed
salt and freshly ground black pepper
2 teaspoons dry sherry
2 teaspoons soy sauce
2 tablespoons oil
Sweet and Sour Sauce
1 (226-g/8-oz) can pineapple chunks
1 carrot, cut into sticks
1 green pepper, seeded and chopped
2 teaspoons brown sugar
2 teaspoons soy sauce
1 tablespoon cornflour
2 tablespoons vinegar

In a bowl mix together the pork, garlic, seasoning, sherry and soy sauce. With floured hands, shape the mixture into walnut-sized balls.

Heat the oil in a frying pan and sauté the meatballs for about 5 minutes, until browned and cooked through. Keep hot.

To make the sweet and sour sauce, drain the juice from the pineapple chunks into a saucepan. Add the carrot and pepper and simmer in the juice for about 5 minutes, or until softened. Stir in the brown sugar and soy sauce. Blend the cornflour to a smooth paste with the vinegar and add to the sauce. Bring to the boil, stirring all the time, and simmer for 2-3 minutes. Stir in the pineapple chunks and let them heat through in the sauce.

Pour the sauce over the meatballs and serve with rice or noodles. *Serves 4*

6
Meatballs and Meat Loaves

Meatballs and meat loaves are universally popular and some of them can be served hot or cold. If serving a meat loaf cold it's a good idea to chill it in the refrigerator as this makes it easier to slice.

A selection of salads goes well with a cold meat loaf, but if serving meatballs and loaves hot I think rice or pasta make good accompaniments and often a sauce is needed too.

If you use non-stick tins there is no need to grease them, but other tins do require a light brushing of oil or melted fat. You don't always have to use a loaf tin – ring the changes and use a ring mould or round (not loose-bottomed) cake tin. If you bake the mixture in a ring mould, when turned out the centre can be filled with rice, pasta or vegetables and a sauce poured over.

Meatballs are traditionally served in many countries under the guise of different names – keftedes in Greece and kofta in India – and you'll find these traditional recipes in the chapter beginning on page 70.

Meatball Fondue

(Illustrated on page 103)

A fondue is an ideal dish for informal entertaining. All the hostess need do is prepare the meatballs, a salad and perhaps some French bread or potatoes baked in their jackets. A selection of chutneys, some ready-prepared mustard and soured cream mixed with chives can be served for the guests to dunk the cooked meatballs into.

450 g / 1 lb minced beef
1 onion, grated
$\frac{1}{4}$ teaspoon grated nutmeg
salt and freshly ground black pepper
pinch of garlic salt
2 tablespoons chopped parsley
1 egg, lightly beaten
flour for coating
pure corn oil for deep frying

In a bowl mix together the beef, onion, nutmeg, seasonings and parsley. Bind the mixture with the lightly beaten egg. With floured hands, shape the mixture into walnut-sized balls and toss lightly in flour. Arrange on a dish in a single layer, cover with cling film and chill, for at least 1 hour, in the refrigerator.

Half fill a metal fondue pan with oil and heat on the cooker. Very carefully carry the pan to the table and place it on the burner. Each guest spears a chilled meatball on a fondue fork and allows it to cook in the heated oil for 1-2 minutes until cooked to his liking, then eats it with the chosen accompaniment. The meatball should not be eaten straight from the fondue fork – it will be very hot.

If the temperature of the oil drops too much and the meatballs don't sizzle immediately they are put into the oil, return the pan to the cooker to reheat it. *Serves 4-6*

Curried Meatballs

450 g / 1 lb minced beef
1 onion, grated
2 teaspoons curry paste
salt and freshly ground black pepper
75 g / 3 oz sultanas
25 g / 1 oz fresh white breadcrumbs
1 egg, lightly beaten
flour for coating
Sauce
2 tablespoons oil
1 green pepper, seeded and chopped
1 onion, peeled and chopped
1 carrot, diced
1 tablespoon curry powder
1 tablespoon flour
1 (227-g/8-oz) can tomatoes
300 ml/½ pint beef stock

In a bowl mix together the beef, onion, curry paste, seasoning, sultanas and breadcrumbs. Bind with the lightly beaten egg. With floured hands, shape the mixture into 12 balls and toss lightly in flour.

Heat the oil in a flameproof casserole and sauté the meatballs until browned on all sides. Remove the meatballs and add the green pepper, onion and carrot to the oil remaining in the casserole. Sauté until softened. Stir in the curry powder and flour and cook for 3-4 minutes, stirring. Stir in the tomatoes with their juice and stock. Bring to the boil, stirring.

Replace the meatballs, cover and cook in a moderate oven (180°C, 350°F, Gas Mark 4) for 45 minutes.

Serve with rice and a selection of side dishes – mango chutney, sliced tomato and onion, and diced cucumber mixed with natural yogurt. *Serves 4*

Meatballs with Noodles

50 g/2 oz butter
1 onion, peeled and chopped
450 g/1 lb minced beef
50 g/2 oz fresh wholemeal breadcrumbs
pinch of dried mixed herbs
1 teaspoon Worcestershire sauce
pinch of dry mustard
salt and freshly ground black pepper
1 egg, lightly beaten
flour for coating
2 tablespoons oil
1 (425-g/15-oz) can tomatoes
pinch of sugar
175 g/6 oz noodles

Heat the butter in a frying pan and sauté the onion until softened. In a bowl mix together the beef, breadcrumbs, mixed herbs, Worcestershire sauce, mustard and seasoning. Mix in the onions and lightly beaten egg.

With floured hands, shape the meat mixture into 12 balls and toss lightly in flour.

Heat the oil in the frying pan and cook the meatballs until browned on all sides and cooked through. Transfer to a serving dish and keep warm.

Pour the fat out of the pan and add the tomatoes with their juice, sugar and seasoning to taste. Return the pan to the heat, bring the tomatoes to the boil, stirring to break up the whole tomatoes. Simmer for 3-4 minutes. Pour over the meatballs.

Cook the noodles in boiling salted water according to the directions on the packet. Drain and serve with the meatballs.
Serves 4

Spanish Meatballs

Without the sauce these meatballs may be served hot as an appetiser. Cook them in shallow oil over a moderate heat for about 15 minutes, turning so that they brown evenly. Place in a serving bowl and spear each one with a cocktail stick.

350 g/12 oz minced beef
salt and freshly ground black pepper
pinch of dried mixed herbs
1 egg, lightly beaten
18 pimiento-stuffed olives
flour
2 tablespoons oil
2 onions, sliced
1 (298-g/10½-oz) can condensed oxtail soup
few drops of Worcestershire sauce

Place the beef in a bowl and mix in the seasoning and herbs. Mix the lightly beaten egg into the beef mixture.

Drain the olives and pat dry with absorbent paper. Divide the beef mixture into 18 even-sized portions and mould one portion around each olive. Coat the meatballs in a little flour.

Heat the oil in a pan and sauté the meatballs until lightly browned on all sides. Remove the meatballs and add the onions to the pan. Sauté until softened. Drain off any excess oil and stir in the soup and Worcestershire sauce. Bring to the boil, then return the meatballs to the pan. Lower the heat, cover and simmer for 20 minutes.

Spoon the meatballs into a serving dish and pour over the sauce. *Serves 3-4*

Oriental Lamb

450 g / 1 lb minced lamb
1 tablespoon chopped fresh thyme
salt and freshly ground black pepper
flour for coating
2 tablespoons oil
1 onion, peeled and sliced
1 aubergine, diced
1 leek, sliced
1 tablespoon flour
1 bay leaf
pinch of ground coriander
2 teaspoons tomato purée
1 (227-g/8-oz) can tomatoes
300 ml/½ pint stock
soured cream or natural yogurt

In a bowl mix together the lamb, thyme and seasoning. With floured hands, shape into 12 balls and toss lightly in flour.

Heat the oil in a flameproof casserole and sauté the meatballs until browned on all sides. Remove the meatballs and add the onion, aubergine and leek to the oil remaining in the casserole. Sauté until softened. Stir in the flour and cook for 1-2 minutes, stirring. Add the bay leaf, coriander, tomato purée and tomatoes with their juice. Gradually add the stock and, stirring, bring the mixture to the boil.

Return the meatballs to the casserole, cover and cook in a moderate oven (160°C, 325°F, Gas Mark 3) for 1 hour.

Remove from the oven, discard the bay leaf and stir in the soured cream or yogurt. Reheat, but do not boil. *Serves 4*

Italian Meatballs

225 g/8 oz minced beef
225 g/8 oz minced veal
1 onion, grated
1 clove garlic, crushed
1 tablespoon chopped parsley
1 tablespoon grated Parmesan cheese
salt and freshly ground black pepper
25 g/1 oz fresh white breadcrumbs
1 egg, lightly beaten
2 tablespoons dry red wine
1 tablespoon oil
50 g/2 oz butter
600 ml/1 pint tomato sauce (see page 123)

In a bowl mix together the beef, veal, onion, garlic, parsley, cheese, seasoning and breadcrumbs. Bind the mixture with the lightly beaten egg and the wine. With floured hands, shape the mixture into 12 balls.

Heat the oil and butter in a flameproof casserole and sauté the meatballs until browned on all sides. Pour off the fat and add the tomato sauce to the casserole. Cover and simmer very gently on top of the cooker for 1 hour; alternatively, cook in a moderate oven (160°C, 325°F, Gas Mark 3) for the same amount of time.

Serve with spaghetti tossed in butter and a grating of nutmeg.
Serves 4

Mushroom-stuffed Loaf

225 g/8 oz mushrooms
25 g/1 oz butter
3 spring onions, chopped
squeeze of lemon juice
50 g/2 oz fresh white breadcrumbs
salt and freshly ground black pepper
2 tablespoons chopped parsley
1 tablespoon chopped fresh thyme
675 g/1½ lb minced beef
1 egg, lightly beaten
3 tablespoons tomato purée
2 tablespoons hot water
pinch of dry mustard

Discard the stems and slice the mushrooms, keeping back a few for the top. Heat the butter in a frying pan and sauté the mushrooms and spring onions for 5 minutes. Stir in the lemon juice, breadcrumbs, seasoning and herbs.

Mix the beef with the lightly beaten egg, tomato purée blended with the hot water, the mustard and seasoning.

Pack half the meat mixture into a greased 1-kg/2-lb loaf tin and spread with the mushroom mixture. Press in the remaining meat mixture and top with the reserved whole mushrooms.

Cook in a moderate oven (180°C, 350°F, Gas Mark 4) for 1¼-1½ hours. Serve hot or cold. *Serves 6-8*

Beef and Aubergine Loaf

(Illustrated on page 104)

2 large aubergines
225 g/8 oz sausagemeat
1 tablespoon Worcestershire sauce
$\frac{1}{2}$ teaspoon dried mixed herbs
1 egg, lightly beaten
450 g/1 lb minced beef
1 onion, grated
2 tablespoons fresh white breadcrumbs
salt and freshly ground black pepper
Garnish
cucumber and radish slices

Using a fork, prick the surface of the aubergines and bake in a moderately hot oven (190°C, 375°F, Gas Mark 5) for about 45 minutes, until softened. Cool under cold water, then peel off the skin. Mash the flesh with a fork or purée in a liquidiser.

Mix the aubergine flesh with the remaining ingredients and pack the mixture into a greased 1-kg/2-lb loaf tin. Cook in a moderate oven (180°C, 350°F, Gas Mark 4) for $1\frac{1}{4}$-$1\frac{1}{2}$ hours. Allow to cool. Turn out, garnish with cucumber and radish slices and serve cold. *Serves 6-8*

Yankee Meat Loaf

50 g/2 oz butter
1 onion, chopped
1 clove garlic, crushed
1 green pepper, seeded and chopped
4 tablespoons red wine
675 g/1½ lb minced beef
50 g/2 oz fresh white breadcrumbs
salt and freshly ground black pepper
1 tablespoon Worcestershire sauce
few drops of Tabasco sauce
2 tablespoons chopped parsley
2 teaspoons chopped fresh thyme
1 teaspoon chopped fresh tarragon
1 egg, lightly beaten
1 tomato, sliced

Heat the butter in a frying pan and sauté the onion, garlic and green pepper for 5 minutes. Add the wine and simmer for 5 minutes, to allow the wine to reduce.

Mix together the beef, breadcrumbs, seasoning, Worcestershire and Tabasco sauces, and the herbs. Stir in the onion mixture and bind with the lightly beaten egg.

Pack the mixture into a greased 1-kg/2-lb loaf tin. Arrange the tomato slices on top and bake in a moderate oven (180°C, 350°F, Gas Mark 4) for 1¼-1½ hours. Serve hot or cold. *Serves 6-8*

Beef and Spinach Loaf

50 g / 2 oz butter
1 onion, chopped
2 sticks celery, chopped
2 (283-g / 10-oz) packets frozen spinach
675 g / 1½ lb minced beef
50 g / 2 oz fresh white breadcrumbs
¼ teaspoon ground nutmeg
salt and freshly ground black pepper
1 egg, lightly beaten
4 rashers streaky bacon

Heat the butter in a frying pan and sauté the onion and celery until softened.

Cook the spinach according to the directions on the packet and *drain well.*

Mix together the beef, softened vegetables, spinach, breadcrumbs, nutmeg and plenty of seasoning. Bind with the lightly beaten egg.

Pack the mixture into a greased 1-kg / 2-lb loaf tin and lay the bacon rashers on top. Cook in a moderate oven (180°C, 350°F, Gas Mark 4) for 1¼-1½ hours.

Serve hot. *Serves 6-8*

Curried Lamb Loaf

350 g/12 oz minced lamb
2 teaspoons curry powder
1 teaspoon curry paste
2 tablespoons mango chutney
1 onion, grated
50 g/2 oz fresh white breadcrumbs
salt and freshly ground black pepper
squeeze of lemon juice
1 egg, lightly beaten
Curry Cream Sauce
25 g/1 oz butter
1 onion, chopped
1-2 teaspoons curry powder
150 ml/$\frac{1}{4}$ pint stock or water
1 (142-ml/5-fl oz) carton single cream

Mix together the lamb, curry powder, curry paste, chutney, onion and breadcrumbs. Season well, add a squeeze of lemon juice and bind the mixture with the lightly beaten egg. Pack into a greased 450-g/1-lb loaf tin and cook in a moderate oven (180°C, 350°F, Gas Mark 4) for about 1$\frac{1}{4}$ hours.

To make the sauce, heat the butter in a pan and sauté the onion until softened. Stir in the curry powder and cook, stirring, for 2-3 minutes. Gradually add the stock, bring to the boil and simmer for 5 minutes. Adjust the seasoning, if necessary, and stir in the cream. Reheat, but do not boil.

Turn the loaf on to a heated serving dish and either spoon over the sauce or serve it separately. *Serves 4*

Speedy Blender Loaf

This really is quick to make. A food processor can take the place of a liquidiser.

1 egg
4 tablespoons red wine
1 clove garlic
4 sprigs parsley
1 onion, chopped
few fresh sage leaves
1 stick celery, chopped
675 g/1½ lb minced veal
225 g/8 oz minced pork
1 tablespoon fresh white breadcrumbs
salt and freshly ground black pepper

Place the egg, wine, garlic, parsley, onion, sage and celery in a liquidiser. Blend until the vegetables are finely chopped.

Mix the meats together in a bowl and stir in the breadcrumbs and vegetable mixture. Season well and pack into a greased 1-kg/2-lb loaf tin. Cook in a moderate oven (180°C, 350°F, Gas Mark 4) for 1¼-1½ hours.

Turn out and serve hot or cold. *Serves 6-8*

Meatball fondue (see page 91)

7

Fork Fare for a Crowd

As well as being versatile, minced meat is one of the least expensive cuts you can buy, making it a doubly suitable choice for feeding a crowd. The food is also easy to eat with a fork – one of the main considerations if you are planning to serve a number of friends informally.

The dishes which take a little longer to prepare can always be prepared and sometimes cooked the day before, providing they are cooled quickly and stored in the refrigerator overnight. Many of the dishes can be cooked and served in the same utensil making the chore of washing up easier.

When planning your party menu, remember to serve a selection of suitable accompaniments. Hot garlic or herb bread always go down well and can take the place of potatoes, rice or pasta. You can choose a seasonal vegetable or a selection of salads. In winter go for a cabbage (Chinese cabbage is excellent) and carrot salad, a Waldorf salad or a pasta salad providing that your main course doesn't contain pasta. In summer try a cucumber and yogurt salad, green salad with fresh herbs or a tomato and onion salad sprinkled with chives. Avoid repeating an ingredient – for example if you choose the Lamb and haricot casserole which contains tomatoes, do not serve a tomato salad as an accompaniment.

Beef and aubergine loaf (see page 98)

105

Beef and Bean Casserole

1 tablespoon oil
2 onions, chopped
1 clove garlic, crushed
450 g / 1 lb minced beef
1 teaspoon chilli powder
salt and freshly ground black pepper
1 (425-g / 15-oz) can tomatoes
1 (432-g / 15¼-oz) can red kidney beans
100 g / 4 oz long-grain rice
1 green pepper, seeded and chopped
100 g / 4 oz stoned green olives
100 g / 4 oz Cheddar cheese, grated

Heat the oil in a flameproof casserole and sauté the onion and garlic for 5 minutes. Stir in the beef and cook until browned. Add the chilli powder, seasoning, the tomatoes and beans with their juices, the rice and green pepper. Bring to the boil, cover and cook in a moderate oven (180°C, 350°F, Gas Mark 4) for 1 hour.

Stir in the olives and cheese and cook for a further 15 minutes. Serve with French bread. *Serves 8*

Pasta and Beef Layer

This party dish can be prepared the day before and left covered with cling film in the refrigerator overnight. The following day it simply needs to be reheated through in a moderate oven.

50 g / 2 oz butter
2 onions, chopped
900 g / 2 lb minced beef
pinch each of ground cinnamon, cloves and allspice
salt and freshly ground black pepper
2 tablespoons tomato purée
150 ml / ¼ pint red wine
450 g / 1 lb pasta shapes
2 eggs, lightly beaten
Cream Sauce
75 g / 3 oz butter
75 g / 3 oz plain flour
salt and freshly ground white pepper
1 litre / 1¾ pints milk
3 eggs, lightly beaten
100 g / 4 oz grated Parmesan cheese

Heat the butter in a large frying pan and sauté the onions until softened. Stir in the beef and seasonings and cook until browned. Add the tomato purée and wine, cover and simmer for 10 minutes.

Cook the pasta according to the directions on the packet. Drain, rinse in cold water, then mix with the beaten eggs.

Make a white sauce with the butter, flour, seasoning and milk. When cooked and thickened, remove from the heat and gradually pour on to the beaten eggs, stirring all the time.

To assemble the dish, spoon half the pasta into a lightly greased large ovenproof dish and sprinkle with one-third of the cheese. Now cover with a layer of the meat mixture and the second third of the cheese followed by the rest of the pasta. Pour the cream sauce over the pasta and sprinkle with the remaining cheese.

Cook in a moderate oven (180°C, 350°F, Gas Mark 4) for 45 minutes-1 hour. Serve from the dish with a selection of salads.
Serves 10-12

Beef and Spinach Pancakes

This is another dish where the fiddly preparation can be done in advance, leaving the final reheating to be done prior to serving.

2 tablespoons oil
2 onions, chopped
2 cloves garlic, crushed
675 g/1½ lb minced beef
450 g/1 lb pork sausagemeat
4 (283-g/10-oz) packets frozen spinach
¼ teaspoon grated nutmeg
salt and freshly ground black pepper
40 pancakes (see Stuffed pancakes, page 55)
1.15 litres/2 pints tomato sauce (see page 123)
225 g/8 oz mature Cheddar cheese, grated

Heat the oil in a large frying pan and sauté the onions and garlic for 5 minutes. Stir in the beef and sauté until browned. Add the sausagemeat and cook, stirring to break up the lumps, until browned. Cover and leave to simmer while the spinach is cooking.

Cook the spinach according to the directions on the packet. *Drain well* and stir in the nutmeg.

Season the meat mixture and mix with the spinach. Leave to cool.

Place some of the filling down the centre of each pancake and fold over the sides and top to enclose the filling. Arrange the filled pancakes in a single layer, seam sides down, in buttered, quite shallow ovenproof dishes.

Cover the pancakes with the tomato sauce and sprinkle the surface with grated cheese.

Cook in a moderate oven (180°C, 350°F, Gas Mark 4) for 40-45 minutes.

Serve with a selection of salads. *Serves 20*

Beef and Courgette Pie

50 g /2 oz butter
2 onions, chopped
450 g /1 lb minced beef
150 ml /¼ pint red wine
225 g /8 oz tomatoes, peeled and sliced
pinch of dried oregano
salt and freshly ground black pepper
4 courgettes
225 g /8 oz puff pastry
beaten egg to glaze

Heat the butter in a frying pan and sauté the onions until softened. Stir in the beef and cook until browned. Add the wine, tomatoes, oregano and seasoning. Cover and simmer for 30 minutes. Leave to cool.

Top, tail and slice the courgettes and arrange half of them in the bottom of a pie dish. Spoon in the beef mixture and cover with the remaining courgettes.

Roll out the pastry and cover the pie. Flake and flute the edges and brush the top with beaten egg. Make some leaves from the pastry trimmings and use to decorate the pie. Glaze the leaves and make a hole in the centre of the pastry.

Bake in a hot oven (220°C, 425°F, Gas Mark 7) for 15 minutes. Reduce the temperature to moderate (180°C, 350°F, Gas Mark 4) and bake for a further 40 minutes, covering the pastry with foil to prevent it becoming too brown. *Serves 6*

Lamb and Haricot Casserole

350 g / 12 oz haricot beans
225 g / 8 oz streaky bacon
2 onions, sliced
2 cloves garlic, crushed
900 g / 2 lb minced lamb
150 ml / ¼ pint dry white wine
1 tablespoon tomato purée
1 (425-g / 15-oz) can tomatoes
1 bay leaf
¼ teaspoon dried marjoram
salt and freshly ground black pepper
1 green pepper, seeded and chopped

Cover the beans with cold water and leave to soak overnight. The following day, cook them in fresh, salted water for 30 minutes. Drain and reserve 450 ml / ¾ pint of the liquor.

Remove the rinds and chop the bacon. Place in a frying pan and sauté until beginning to crisp. Remove with a draining spoon. Sauté the onions and garlic in the bacon fat until softened. Stir in the lamb and cook until browned.

Place the bacon, lamb mixture, beans, bean liquor and wine in a flameproof casserole. Add the tomato purée, tomatoes with their juice, herbs and plenty of seasoning.

Bring to the boil on top of the cooker, then cover and cook in a moderate oven (180°C, 350°F, Gas Mark 4) for 1 hour. Add the green pepper and cook for a further 30 minutes. Adjust the seasoning, if necessary, and serve. *Serves 6-8*

Moussaka

Here's another version of moussaka, this one with a sauce topping. Again, the dish can be assembled the day before it is required.

450 g / 1 lb aubergines
salt
4 tablespoons oil
2 onions, chopped
2 cloves garlic, crushed
1 kg / 2 lb minced lamb
$\frac{1}{2}$ teaspoon dried marjoram
1 (227-g / 8-oz) can tomatoes
150 ml / $\frac{1}{4}$ pint red wine
salt and freshly ground black pepper
600 ml / 1 pint tomato sauce (see page 123)
Topping
1 egg
50 g / 2 oz Parmesan cheese, grated
pinch of grated nutmeg
300 ml / $\frac{1}{2}$ pint white sauce

Slice the aubergines and place in a single layer on a large plate. Sprinkle with salt and leave for 1 hour.

Heat half the oil in a pan and sauté the onions and garlic until softened. Add the lamb and sauté until browned. Add the marjoram, tomatoes with their juice, wine and seasoning and simmer for 15 minutes.

Meanwhile, rinse the aubergine slices in cold water and pat dry with absorbent paper. Heat the remaining oil in a frying pan and fry the aubergine slices, a few at a time, until lightly browned on both sides. Drain on absorbent paper.

To assemble the dish, arrange a layer of aubergine slices in the bottom of an oiled ovenproof dish. Now add the lamb and tomato sauce in alternating layers and finish with a layer of aubergines.

Beat the egg, cheese and nutmeg into the white sauce. Pour over the aubergines and cook in a moderate oven (180°C, 350°F, Gas Mark 4) for 45 minutes. *Serves 6*

Minced Lamb Hot Pot

3 tablespoons oil
4 onions, sliced
1.5 kg / 3 lb minced lamb
1 kg / 2 lb potatoes, sliced
salt and freshly ground black pepper
pinch of dried thyme
pinch of dried rosemary
1 bay leaf
300 ml / ½ pint dry white wine

Heat 2 tablespoons of the oil in a frying pan and sauté the onions until softened. Transfer the onions to a plate.

Add the remaining oil to the frying pan, heat and brown the lamb, stirring.

Arrange half the onions in a layer in the bottom of a large flameproof casserole, followed by a layer of half the potato slices. Season well. Cover with the meat and add the thyme, rosemary, bay leaf and more seasoning.

Cover the meat with the rest of the onions and top with the remaining potatoes. Season lightly and pour in the wine.

Cover the casserole with a tight-fitting lid and bring to the boil on top of the cooker. Place in a moderate oven (180°C, 350°F, Gas Mark 4) and cook for 1-1¼ hours, removing the lid for the last 15 minutes cooking time to allow the potatoes to brown.
Serves 8

Minced Lamb Korma

*Served with a selection of traditional curry accompaniments,
this recipe is a winner at any party.*

1.5 kg/3 lb minced lamb
1 (284-ml/10-fl oz) carton natural yogurt
½ teaspoon ground cardamom
1 teaspoon ground cumin
1½ teaspoons ground turmeric
100 g/4 oz fresh coconut flesh, grated
300 ml/½ pint water
4 tablespoons oil
3 onions, sliced
2 cloves garlic, crushed
4 tomatoes, peeled and sliced
pinch of ground ginger
4 cloves
pinch of cayenne
1 cinnamon stick
1 bay leaf
salt and freshly ground black pepper
grated rind and juice of ½ lemon

Place the lamb in a bowl and pour over the yogurt mixed with cardamom, cumin and turmeric. Stir well so that all the lamb is coated with the yogurt mixture. Cover with cling film and leave in the refrigerator for 1 hour.

Place the grated coconut in a pan with the water. Bring to the boil and simmer for 15 minutes. Strain off the liquor and reserve.

Heat the oil in a flameproof casserole and sauté the onions and garlic until softened. Add the lamb mixture and tomatoes and simmer for 5 minutes, stirring. Stir in the ginger, cloves and cayenne and add the cinnamon stick, bay leaf and plenty of seasoning.

Pour in the reserved coconut milk, bring to the boil, cover and simmer for 1 hour. Towards the end of the cooking remove the lid to allow the excess liquid to evaporate. Discard the bay leaf and cinnamon stick, stir in the lemon rind and juice and adjust the seasoning. Serve with rice. *Serves 8*

Lamb Pilaff

50 g / 2 oz butter
3 onions, sliced
675 g / 1½ lb minced lamb
50 g / 2 oz pine nuts
50 g / 2 oz raisins
225 g / 8 oz long-grain rice
2 tomatoes, peeled and sliced
900 ml / 1½ pints light stock or water
2 tablespoons chopped parsley
½ teaspoon dried sage
¼ teaspoon ground coriander
¼ teaspoon ground cinnamon
salt and freshly ground black pepper
Garnish
chopped parsley

Heat the butter in a flameproof casserole and sauté the onions until softened. Add the lamb and sauté until browned. Stir in the pine nuts, raisins, rice and tomatoes. Add the stock, herbs, spices and seasoning. Bring to the boil, lower the heat, cover and simmer very gently for about 25 minutes, until the rice is tender and the liquid absorbed.

Remove the lid and fork the mixture over the heat to dry off any excess moisture.

Turn into a serving dish and garnish with chopped parsley. Serve with a selection of salads. *Serves 6*

Tourtière

This is a savoury pork pie topped with a puff pastry crust which can be prepared in advance. The recipe is sufficient for 2 pies; if you wish to make only 1, simply halve the quantities.

2 tablespoons oil
1 onion, chopped
1 clove garlic, crushed
2 sticks celery, chopped
1.5 kg/3 lb minced pork
4 tablespoons chopped parsley
pinch each of mace and marjoram
salt and freshly ground black pepper
pinch of cayenne
150 ml/$\frac{1}{4}$ pint dry cider
2 bay leaves
350 g/12 oz puff pastry
beaten egg to glaze

Heat the oil in a large frying pan and sauté the onion, garlic and celery for 5 minutes. Stir in the pork and cook until browned. Mix in the parsley, herbs, seasonings and cider. Cover and simmer over a moderate heat for 30 minutes. Leave to cool.

Spoon the pork mixture into two 25-cm/10-inch pie dishes and add a bay leaf to each. Halve the pastry and roll each half into a round large enough to cover the filling. Place over the filling, then flake and flute the edges. Brush with beaten egg and make a hole in the centre for the steam to escape.

Bake in a hot oven (220°C, 425°F, Gas Mark 7) for 15 minutes. Reduce the temperature to moderate (180°C, 350°F, Gas Mark 4) and bake for a further 30-35 minutes, covering the pastry with foil to prevent it from becoming too brown.

Serve hot. *Serves 16-20*

Pork and Spinach Loaf

This needs to be made the day before it is required. A Waldorf salad is a good accompaniment to this pork loaf.

about 10 rashers streaky bacon
2 bay leaves
1 (283-g/10-oz) packet frozen spinach
350 g/12 oz minced pork
225 g/8 oz sausagemeat
1 onion, grated
2 cloves garlic, crushed
salt and freshly ground black pepper
pinch of ground nutmeg
1 tablespoon chopped parsley
1 tablespoon chopped fresh mixed herbs
1 egg, lightly beaten
Garnish
gherkin fans

Remove the bacon rinds and stretch the rashers. Place the bay leaves in the bottom of a greased 1-kg/2-lb loaf tin and line the tin with the bacon.

Cook the spinach according to the directions on the packet and drain well. Mix with the pork, sausagemeat, onion and garlic. Season the mixture, stir in the nutmeg, parsley and herbs and bind with the egg. Pack into the lined loaf tin and press the mixture down well. Cover with foil and place in a roasting tin with water half-way up the sides. Cook in a moderately hot oven (190°C, 375°F, Gas Mark 5) for 2 hours.

Leave to cool in the tin, weighted. Turn out, cover with cling film and chill overnight. Serve garnished with gherkin fans. *Serves 6-8*

Pork, Aubergine and Apple Bake

2 tablespoons oil
3 onions, sliced
675 g/1½ lb minced pork
1 (425-g/15-oz) can tomatoes
150 ml/¼ pint dry cider
salt and freshly ground black pepper
2 sprigs rosemary
2 cooking apples, peeled, cored and sliced
1 aubergine, sliced
Topping
1 (142-ml/5-fl oz) soured cream

Heat the oil in a frying pan and sauté the onions until softened. Remove to a plate. Add the pork to the pan and cook, stirring, until browned. Add the tomatoes with their juice and the cider. Bring to the boil and season well.

Place half the onions in a layer in the bottom of an ovenproof dish. Cover with half the pork mixture, adding a sprig of rosemary, followed by a layer of the apples and aubergine. Add the final layer of onions and top with the remaining pork mixture. Add the other sprig of rosemary, cover and cook in a moderate oven (160°C, 325°F, Gas Mark 3) for 1½-2 hours.

Adjust the seasoning, if necessary, and spoon the soured cream over the top. Return to the oven for a further 5 minutes. Serve with pasta. *Serves 6*

8

Sauces

Sauces are as important as the dish itself and, contrary to popular belief, there is no mystique in their making.

All the sauces in this chapter, apart from béarnaise, are good freezer candidates so are worth making in bulk and freezing in usable portions. I find that the boilable bags are good for freezing sauces as they can be reheated in a pan of boiling water, which saves you standing over a pan containing a block of frozen sauce and jabbing at it until it reluctantly begins to defrost!

When making the keftede sauce which uses fresh tomatoes it is essential that the tomatoes are peeled – there's nothing worse than trying to extract those nasty curled up tomato skins from the cooked sauce. The quickest and easiest way to peel an amount of tomatoes is to place them in a bowl and cover with boiling water. Leave for 1-2 minutes until the skins split, then remove them one at a time and with a small vegetable knife quickly peel away the skins.

Bolognaise Sauce

This is the well-known Italian sauce which accompanies pasta, or is used in the making of lasagne. It does freeze well and is worth making in quantity to freeze and use when you need to produce an instant meal – perfectly cooked pasta tossed in butter, served with Bolognaise sauce and grated Parmesan cheese makes an instant meal to be proud of.

3 rashers bacon
50 g / 2 oz butter
1 onion, chopped
1 clove garlic, crushed
2 carrots, chopped
2 sticks celery, chopped
225 g / 8 oz minced beef
100 g / 4 oz minced pork
100 g / 4 oz minced veal
1 (227-g / 8-oz) can tomatoes
150 ml / $\frac{1}{4}$ pint chicken stock
150 ml / $\frac{1}{4}$ pint red wine
2 tablespoons tomato purée
pinch of ground nutmeg
225 g / 8 oz mushrooms, sliced
salt and freshly ground black pepper
4 tablespoons double cream

Remove the rinds and chop the bacon. Heat the butter in a pan and sauté the bacon for 2 minutes. Add the onion, garlic, carrots and celery and sauté until the vegetables are beginning to soften. Add the meats and sauté, stirring, until browned on all sides. Add the tomatoes with their juice, stock, wine, tomato purée, nutmeg, mushrooms and seasoning. Cover and simmer for 1 hour.

Stir in the cream just before serving. *Serves 6*

Note Omit the cream when freezing the sauce. Stir it in at the reheating stage.

Béarnaise Sauce

This classic sauce can be served with burgers to elevate them to dinner party status.

2 teaspoons chopped shallot
2 sprigs tarragon
2 sprigs chervil
2 peppercorns, crushed
3 tablespoons tarragon vinegar
6 tablespoons dry white wine
3 egg yolks
175 g / 6 oz butter, at room temperature
salt and freshly ground white pepper
pinch of cayenne

Place the shallot, tarragon, chervil, peppercorns, vinegar and wine in a small pan. Simmer over a moderate heat until the liquid is reduced to two-thirds of the original quantity. Cool slightly.

Put the egg yolks in a basin placed over a pan of hot water and add the slightly cooled shallot mixture. Whisk until the mixture is light and fluffy, taking care that the water does not boil.

Whisking all the time, add the butter, bit by bit. Continue whisking until the sauce thickens.

Strain, season to taste and serve.

Note The sauce can be made a little while before serving in which case it can be kept warm over hot water.

A slightly less fraught way to make this sauce is to do it in a liquidiser. Prepare the shallot mixture as above and strain it. Melt the butter, but do not let it brown. Place the egg yolks and seasonings in the goblet and switch on. Pour in the butter in a steady stream. Blend until the mixture has emulsified. Finally, blend in the shallot mixture. *Serves 4-6*

Barbecue Sauce

As well as serving this sauce with burgers and meatballs cooked over the barbecue, it can also go with meat loaves and kebabs.

2 tablespoons oil
1 onion, chopped
150 ml/$\frac{1}{4}$ pint tomato ketchup
150 ml/$\frac{1}{4}$ pint water
3 tablespoons wine vinegar
2 teaspoons made mustard
2 tablespoons soft brown sugar
salt and freshly ground black pepper
2 tablespoons Worcestershire sauce
few drops of Tabasco sauce
1 tablespoon tomato purée

Heat the oil in a pan and sauté the onion until softened. Stir in the remaining ingredients, bring to the boil, cover and simmer for 5 minutes. Remove the lid and cook for a further 2-3 minutes to reduce and thicken the sauce. *Makes about 300 ml/$\frac{1}{2}$ pint*

Kefta Sauce

This sauce is made with fresh tomatoes and is served with Greek keftedes.

450 g / 1 lb tomatoes
25 g / 1 oz butter
1 stick celery, chopped
1 onion, chopped
1 clove garlic, crushed
300 ml / ½ pint water
2 tablespoons chopped parsley
1 tablespoon chopped fresh marjoram
salt and freshly ground black pepper
pinch of paprika
pinch of cayenne

Peel and chop the tomatoes. Heat the butter in a pan and sauté the celery, onion and garlic until softened. Stir in the remaining ingredients and leave the sauce to simmer, uncovered, for about 45 minutes. *Makes about 300 ml / ½ pint*

Tomato Sauce

This sauce can be served with stuffed vegetables, burgers, meatballs, meat loaves and used to make dishes such as cannelloni. Again, this is a good freezer candidate and worth making in bulk.

1 tablespoon oil
1 onion, sliced
2 cloves garlic, crushed
1 (425-g/15-oz) can tomatoes
2 tablespoons tomato purée
1 bay leaf
sprig each of rosemary and thyme
salt and freshly ground black pepper
150 ml/$\frac{1}{4}$ pint chicken stock
25 g/1 oz butter

Heat the oil in a pan and sauté the onion and garlic until softened. Add the tomatoes with their juice, tomato purée, herbs, seasoning and stock. Bring to the boil, cover and simmer for about 45 minutes.

Allow the sauce to cool slightly. Remove the herbs, then blend in a liquidiser or press through a sieve. Adjust the seasoning, if necessary, reheat and enrich with the butter.
Makes about 450 ml/$\frac{3}{4}$ pint

Spanish Sauce

This sauce goes well with burgers, meatballs and meat loaves.

2 tablespoons oil
1 onion, chopped
1 green pepper, seeded and chopped
1 clove garlic, crushed
1 (425-g/15-oz) can tomatoes
1 bay leaf
salt and freshly ground black pepper
50 g/2 oz pimiento-stuffed olives, sliced

Heat the oil in a pan and sauté the onion, green pepper and garlic until softened. Add the tomatoes with their juice, bay leaf and seasoning. Bring to the boil, cover and simmer for about 30 minutes.

Remove the bay leaf, adjust the seasoning, if necessary, and stir in the olives. Simmer for a further 5 minutes, uncovered.
Makes about 300 ml/½ pint

Index

Pork and olive pâté 21
Pork pasties 64
Pork roll en croûte 65
Pork and spinach loaf 116
Pork terrine 20
Stuffed mushrooms 19
Tourtière 115
Puddings:
  Beef and carrot pudding 50
  Scottish pudding 67

Samosas 83
Sauces:
  Barbecue sauce 121
  Béarnaise sauce 120
  Béchamel sauce 75
  Bolognaise sauce 119
  Cheesy mustard sauce 58
  Cream sauce 107
  Curry cream sauce 101
  Egg and lemon sauce 81
  Kefta sauce 122
  Pizzaiola sauce 29
  Spanish sauce 124
  Sweet and sour sauce 89
  Tomato sauce 123
Sausage, home-made 66
Scottish pudding 67
Soup:
  Beef soup 23
  Italian meatball soup 25
  Mexican soup 24

Spanish meatballs 94
Spanish sauce 124
Spicy dip 16
Steak tartare 72
Storing minced meats 11
Stuffed marrow 58
Stuffed mushrooms 19
Stuffed pancakes 55
Stuffed tomatoes 18
Suet pastry 67
Sweet and sour sauce 89

Terrine of pork 20
Texas hash 56
Tomato sauce 123
Tomatoes, stuffed 18
Tourtière 115
Turkish kebabs 80

Veal:
  Hungarian veal 87
  Picnic pie 69
  Veal roll 68
  Veal-stuffed cannelloni 84

West Country pie 48
Wine-glazed burgers 37